Studies in African American History and Culture

Edited by
Graham Hodges
Colgate University

A Routledge Series

Studies in African American History and Culture

Graham Hodges, *General Editor*

Constructing Belonging
Class, Race, and Harlem's Professional Workers
Sabiyha Prince

Contesting the Terrain of the Ivory Tower
Spiritual Leadership of African-American Women in the Academy
Rochelle Garner

Post-Soul Black Cinema
Discontinuities, Innovations, and Breakpoints, 1970–1995
William R. Grant, IV

The Mysterious Voodoo Queen, Marie Laveaux
A Study of Powerful Female Leadership in Nineteenth-Century New Orleans
Ina Johanna Fandrich

Race and Masculinity in Contemporary American Prison Narratives
Auli Ek

Swinging the Vernacular
Jazz and African American Modernist Literature
Michael Borshuk

Boys, Boyz, Bois
An Ethics of Black Masculinity in Film and Popular Media
Keith M. Harris

Movement Matters
American Antiapartheid Activism and the Rise of Multicultural Politics
David L. Hostetter

Slavery, Southern Culture, and Education in Little Dixie, Missouri, 1820–1860
Jeffrey C. Stone

Courting Communities
Black Female Nationalism and "Syncre-Nationalism" in the Nineteenth-Century North
Kathy L. Glass

The Selling of Civil Rights
The Student Nonviolent Coordinating Committee and the Use of Public Relations
Vanessa Murphree

Black Liberation in the Midwest
The Struggle in St. Louis, Missouri, 1964–1970
Kenneth S. Jolly

When to Stop the Cheering?
The Black Press, the Black Community, and the Integration of Professional Baseball
Brian Carroll

The Rise and Fall of the Garvey Movement in the Urban South, 1918–1942
Claudrena N. Harold

The Black Panthers in the Midwest
The Community Programs and Services of the Black Panther Party in Milwaukee, 1966–1977
Andrew Witt

THE BLACK PANTHERS IN THE MIDWEST

The Community Programs and Services of the Black Panther Party in Milwaukee, 1966-1977

Andrew Witt

Routledge
New York & London

Routledge
Taylor & Francis Group
270 Madison Avenue
New York, NY 10016

Routledge
Taylor & Francis Group
2 Park Square
Milton Park, Abingdon
Oxon OX14 4RN

© 2007 by Taylor & Francis Group, LLC
Routledge is an imprint of Taylor & Francis Group, an Informa business

Printed in the United States of America on acid-free paper
10 9 8 7 6 5 4 3 2 1

International Standard Book Number-10: 0-415-98148-4 (Hardcover)
International Standard Book Number-13: 978-0-415-98148-4 (Hardcover)

Library of Congress Cataloging-in-Publication Data

Witt, Andrew, 1974-
   The Black Panthers in the Midwest : the community programs and services of the Black Panther Party in Milwaukee, 1966-1977 / Andrew Witt.
      p. cm. -- (Studies in African American history and culture)
   Includes bibliographical references and index.
   ISBN 978-0-415-98148-4
   1. African Americans--Wisconsin--Milwaukee--Politics and government--20th century. 2. Black Panther Party--History. 3. African Americans--Civil rights--Wisconsin--Milwaukee--History--20th century. 4. African Americans--Services for--Wisconsin--Milwaukee--History--20th century. 5. Community life--Wisconsin--Milwaukee--Social conditions--20th century. 6. African Americans--Wisconsin--Milwaukee--Social conditions--20th century. 7. Milwaukee (Wis.)--Race relations--History--20th century. 8. Milwaukee (Wis.)--Social conditions--20th century. I. Title.

F589.M69N48 2007
322.4'20973077595--dc22   2006038302

Visit the Taylor & Francis Web site at
http://www.taylorandfrancis.com

and the Routledge Web site at
http://www.routledge-ny.com

In memory of Richard Witt and Florence Lauscher

Contents

Acknowledgments   ix

Introduction   1

Chapter One
Picking up the Gun and Serving the People   13

Chapter Two
To Serve and Protect   27

Chapter Three
The Black Panther Party in Milwaukee: A Case Study   41

Chapter Four
Providing for All   57

Chapter Five
Leading by Example   71

Chapter Six
Romanticizing the Past?   81

Conclusion   87

Epilogue   91

Appendix A
The 10-Point Program of the Black Panther Party   95

Appendix B
Rules of the Black Panther Party 99

Appendix C
Membership of the Milwaukee Branch 103

Appendix D
A Proposal of the Milwaukee Branch for Community Control of the
Milwaukee Police Department 107

Appendix E
A Sampling of Locations of Black Panther Party Community Programs
Nationwide 111

Notes 115

Bibliography 139

Index 149

Acknowledgments

There are countless individuals whom I would like to thank for helping me get to this point. First, I would like to thank all of those who have helped me throughout my academic career. William Van Deburg introduced me, and thousands of other undergraduates, to African American studies. Tim Tyson showed me that it was acceptable to be passionate when teaching your subject material, and he also helped me to become a more concise writer. Walter Weare helped to mold me into a historian, and he also bore the brunt of answering my early questions surrounding the Black Panther Party. For that, as well as for editing countless drafts for my Master's Thesis, I am deeply indebted to him.

During my first year of pursuing my doctorate at Loyola, I often thought of Tim Tyson's words in *Radio Free Dixie*, where he "daily threatened to flee" his graduate school, because of its demanding nature. Fortunately, I once again found excellent and personable professors who helped guide me through graduate school. Illustrating her devotion to her students, Cheryl Johnson-Odim worked on my major exam and dissertation committees, even though she had moved on to another institution of higher learning. I cringed when Tim Gilfoyle gave me his reading list for my major exam, and now I thank him for it. Gilfoyle is also perhaps the most prompt and thorough scholar that I have ever encountered.

And then there's Paula. Paula Pfeffer put up with my antics for close to six years, which could be why she is retiring this year. In all seriousness, I do not think I could have made it through my graduate studies without Paula's expert guidance and advice. Thank you Paula.

In addition to the numerous individuals who have helped me within academia, there have been countless others outside of academia to whom I owe a lot. Dan Gray served as my first "editor" while at the University of Wisconsin-Milwaukee, and that was a thankless and dreary task. I suppose that could explain why he moved back home to England shortly after finishing his degree. I also owe a lot of thanks to my brother Bill, and sisters Elizabeth and Katy, and my friends and in-laws, Pat and Mark Mato, who cheered me on during this very long journey.

I am especially grateful to my mother, Jane, who made it possible for me to go to college in the first place. I will never forget the sacrifices she endured so that I could get an education.

I would like to thank my baby, Sadie, for making me laugh, even after I missed various publishing deadlines. I hope you will read this someday Sadie, and come to the conclusion that your father actually has an intelligent thought or two.

Finally, I would like to thank Kristin Witt. She is my best friend, wife, and mother of our first-born. No mere words of thanks can adequately express what she means to me, as she means everything to me.

Introduction

In a 2003 interview, former Milwaukee Black Panther leader, and current Commander of the Black Panther Militia, Michael McGee, was asked what he considered the main objective of the Black Panther Party. McGee responded by stating that the central mission of the Party was in providing community programs and services to the African American community. McGee added, "It (the Black Panther Party) was about picking up the hammer. We used to pick up the hammer more than we did the gun."[1]

Historian Arwin D. Smallwood confirms McGee's point when he states, "The Party was established with two major purposes. One was to protect blacks from abuse by the police and the other was to help feed and educate black children who were living in the inner city."[2] And according to Panther co-founder, Huey Newton, the sole reason that the Panthers existed was to "serve the people."[3] Many earlier works dealing with the Panthers have failed to recognize the importance of their services, and some people have referred to the Panthers' attempts as simply, "band-aid" solutions.[4] Regardless of judgments on the success of the Party in providing for the community, the efforts to do so clearly illustrated a large group of individuals who fought for the betterment of the black community, despite facing harassment, beatings, and even death.

The Black Panthers in the Midwest analyzes the community programs of the Milwaukee Black Panther Party, and aims to dispel many of the existing stereotypes about the Party. Misconceptions of the Party range from its being an organization perceived as bent on the violent destruction of the United States, to an overwhelmingly sexist one. This work challenges such stereotypes by examining the community programs of the Party, and the role of women in the Party. The Party was not an extremist group principally dedicated to overthrowing the government of the United States, but rather it was an organization committed to providing essential community services for lower-income and working-class African American communities around the nation. My argument substantially differs from most interpretations of the Party that only conceptualize the Panthers in terms of guns, violence, court cases, and militant rhetoric.

In addition, *The Black Panthers in the Midwest* examines the tradition of armed self-defense and community self-help present in many African American communities. By placing the Panthers in this historical framework, it becomes much more difficult to dismiss the Black Panthers as an aberration or minor phenomenon in the history of African American protest. The Panthers' stance on armed self-defense was representative of a large segment of the African American population that was willing to engage in armed self-defense. The Panthers, however, practiced self-defense on a much wider scale than previous black militants, as evidenced by the sheer number of armed Panther members. In large part, the Panthers' relative success can be attributed to the spirit of the 1960s which witnessed the radicalization of many Americans. Previous African American militants never counted on substantial support from whites, but the Panthers could, as illustrated by the "Free Huey," "Free Angela Davis," "Free the New York Twenty-One" and "Free the Milwaukee Three" campaigns, to name a few.[5] The Panthers also had numerous coalitions with white organizations such as Students for a Democratic Society (SDS), the Peace and Freedom Party (PFP), the Youth International Party (Yippies) and the White Panther Party.[6] In the context of the Sixties, radical whites were drawn to the militant Panthers, and their emphasis on an all-inclusive class struggle.[7]

This book also seeks to partially address the silence in the current literature examining the community programs of the Party. In addition to the lack of information dealing with the programs, what little has been written is plagued with inaccuracies and outright falsehoods. By offering readers well-documented information that counters the stereotypical image of the Panthers, *The Black Panthers in the Midwest* will challenge misconceptions about Black Power itself. Although this work only deals with one particular Black Power group, it is my hope that this work will serve as a gateway to a more complete understanding of the Black Power Movement as a whole.

Most Americans have been exposed to only one side of the Panthers, their militant, misunderstood, political side. The media and the Federal Bureau of Investigation (FBI) portrayed the Panthers as consumed with the idea of violently overthrowing the government of the United States.[8] The Black Panther Party offered much more than inflammatory rhetoric, evidenced by the variety and scope of the humanitarian programs and services they provided. The Black Panthers did employ a militant approach, but they did so in order to adequately defend themselves and their communities from rampant police brutality.

Numerous other studies and reports about the Panthers were, and are still, inaccurate. Former Chief of Staff of the Panthers, David Hilliard, affirms this point of view when he states, "The story of the Black Panther Party has been distorted, forgotten, and repressed over the last twenty years."[9] Works by journalists such as Don A. Schanche's *The Panther Paradox: A Liberal's Dilemma* (1970) and Norman Hill's *Black Panther Menace: America's Neo-Nazis* (1971) are representative of the slanders that plagued the Party in its early years. Schanche stated that the Panther's "thirst for retributive suicide appears in everything the Panthers do," including their Breakfast for Children Program.[10] Schanche closed his work by writing, "The military tradition of the Black Panthers, whom we ourselves have driven to their madness, will spread, and not just the revolutionaries, but all of us, will be doomed."[11] Hill continued this sensationalistic and damning critique of the Panthers by writing that the Panthers were "a totalitarian organization dedicated to violence and dictatorship," and that they practiced, "Nazi-like racism bordering on genocide."[12]

Contemporary works focusing on the Panthers have not progressed very far from earlier interpretations either. John George's and Laird Wilcox's *Nazis, Communists, Klansmen and Others on the Fringe* (1992) focuses strictly on the guns and negative elements of the Party. And as scholar Errol Anthony asserts, Hugh Pearson's *The Shadow of the Black Panther* (1996) indicts the entire Black Panther Party for some of the personal failures of Huey Newton.[13] Movies like *Higher Learning* (1995) and an NBC miniseries entitled, *The Sixties* (1999) also have aided in the misunderstanding of the Panthers. In *Higher Learning*, a student states that the Panthers practice "reverse racism" without any further discussion of the topic.[14] *The Sixties* also projected a highly distorted image of the Panthers. For instance, *The Sixties* portrayed Bobby Seale denouncing another African American for dancing with a "white bitch," even though the Panthers had numerous alliances with white organizations. *The Sixties* also failed to classify the breakfast programs as Black Panther Party Breakfast Programs. One program was referred to as "Fred Hampton's Breakfast Program," and another as the "Children's Breakfast Program in Watts," although both were Panther programs.[15] Filmmakers of *The Sixties* went out of their way to avoid portraying the Panthers in a positive light.

Yet another example of poor treatment of the Black Panther Party is John A. Wood's *The Panthers and the Militias: Brothers Under the Skin?* (2002). One major problem with Wood is that he lumps all black militants from the sixties into a group known as "Panthers." Wood says in his work

that the term "Panther," refers to "any and all 'black militants' in the 1960s
and 1970s who refused to renounce violence as a way to bring about fundamental change in American society."[16] To begin with, the Panthers believed
in armed self-defense, not violence. Wood, however, like many other scholars, views the two terms as interchangeable.[17] Furthermore, under Wood's
overly simplistic classification system of black militants, members of "Us,"
a cultural nationalist organization, who were archenemies of the Party,
would be considered Panthers.

Wood also paints the Panthers as paranoid, as he claims that "some
black militants talked of a conspiracy in more general terms, believing that
law enforcement agencies from the FBI to local sheriffs were conspiring
to deny them basic rights."[18] If Wood had any grounding in the history
of the Civil Rights Movement and Black Power, he would realize that J.
Edgar Hoover's COINTELPRO (Counter-Intelligence Program) was indeed
designed to cripple Civil Rights and Black Power organizations.

There are a handful of new works dealing with the Party that are
offering a more complete, analytical view of the Party. For instance, Charles
Jones's edited work, *The Black Panther Party: Reconsidered* (1998) offers a
favorable and thorough analysis of the Party by examining different aspects
of the Panthers ranging from ideology to gender relations within the Party.
None of the eighteen essays in this work, however, seek to analyze the Party
on the local level, and, only one gives significant attention to the Party's
community programs.[19]

Kathleen Cleaver and George Katsiaficas edited work, *Liberation,
Imagination and the Black Panther Party* (2001) is similar to Jones's study
in that it compiles revisionist essays designed to strengthen our understanding of the Party. As with *The Black Panther Party: Reconsidered*, however,
none of the essays offer an in-depth focus of a particular branch of the
Party. Furthermore, scant attention is given to the community programs of
the Party. Edited works such as *The Black Panther Party: Reconsidered* and
Liberation, Imagination and the Black Panther Party are essential tools for
anyone studying the Panthers because they expose the reader to a variety of
different issues and viewpoints concerning the Party. Yet, these fail to offer
the comprehensive analysis of the Party possible with a monograph.

I have chosen to examine the Black Panther Party for a number
of reasons. First, to document and provide empirical data about a
revolutionary Black Power group which remains misunderstood by most
Americans. To many white Americans, the Black Panther Party represents
the "bogeyman," the most frightening and offensive element within the
Black Power Movement. The popular image of the Party is that of a group
who wanted to shoot police officers and Presidents and instill general

hysteria. Inaccurate assessments of the Panthers not only perpetuate negative stereotypes, but they represent a disservice to the men and women of the Party who fought for their beliefs. While my work may not invalidate all the popular wrongful stereotypes that surround the Black Panthers, it will contribute to a more scholarly base from which a clearer understanding of the Black Panther Party may emerge.

The many misconceptions surrounding the Party exist for a number of reasons. First, the Party openly armed themselves, and as a result, the Panthers became a "mainstay" of the media.[20] Images of armed black men and women were routinely displayed on television and in the newspaper, with no explanations offered as to why the Panthers carried guns. In addition to arming themselves, the Party employed militant rhetoric, such as the use of the phrase, "offing the Pig." Statements such as this caused many people to believe that the Panthers wanted to kill all cops. The Panthers, however, made it clear that a "Pig" was not just any police officer, but any police officer who brutalized the African American community.[21]

Contributing to the shallow understanding of the Party was their decision to bar whites from membership. Many liberal whites could not fathom why Black Power groups chose to exclude whites, and as journalist Jonathan Coleman writes, "The inherent problem with being...a white liberal is this: If you don't feel appreciated, you feel resentful."[22] Consequently, numerous liberal whites tended to view Black Power, and the Party, through a lens clouded with their own personal biases, further contributing to the misunderstanding of the Party. Stokely Carmichael solidifies this point when he writes "whenever black people have moved toward genuinely independent action, the society has distorted their intentions or damned their performance."[23]

The Panthers did exclude whites from membership within their own organization mainly for purposes of control and self-esteem, for much the same reasons as earlier Black Power-type movements. For instance, A. Philip Randolph's March on Washington Movement of 1941 was all-black, because according to Randolph:

> The essential value of an all-Negro movement...is that it helps to create faith by Negroes in Negroes. It develops a sense of self-reliance with Negroes depending on Negroes in vital matters. It helps to break down the slave psychology and inferiority-complex in Negroes which comes and is nourished with Negroes relying on white people for direction and support.[24]

Black Panther Party co-founder Huey Newton argued that the Panthers should have all-black membership because:

Every ethnic group has particular needs that they know and understand better than anybody else; each group is the best judge of how its institutions ought to affect the lives of its members. Throughout American history ethnic groups like the Irish and Italians have established organizations and institutions within their own communities.[25]

The Black Panthers were also operating in the context of Black Power, when many African Americans believed they needed to have "the power to control their own destinies."[26]

In order to control their own destiny, the Panthers concluded that they could not have whites within their ranks.

Furthermore, the Black Panther Party wanted to avert some of the problems that plagued interracial groups like the Student Non-violent Coordinating Committee (SNCC). For instance, SNCC experienced huge rifts as a result of its Freedom Summer Movement in 1964. During Freedom Summer roughly 700-800 whites were recruited by SNCC to come to Mississippi to engage in grassroots organizing. Many African American SNCC staffers and local black Mississippians, however, began to notice that these white volunteers were often bossy, and some feared they sought to take over the movement.[27] Numerous black activists were tired of whites joining various organizations and assuming leadership positions only because they enjoyed more formal educations. And then a number of these same white liberals defected from the Civil Rights Movement to join other movements or causes, such as the Anti-War or Free Speech Movements in 1964-1965, leaving a bitter taste in the mouths of numerous African American activists.[28] How committed and dependable were white liberals who could just abandon a movement for another movement at such short notice? The Black Panther Party did not put themselves in a position to find out.

And finally, the Party is poorly understood because of racism. Numerous historians, journalists, television stations, and society in general, have allowed racism to pervade their understanding of the Party. Bigots condemned and distorted the image of less controversial figures like Martin Luther King, Jr., so it should not be surprising that the militant Party has had its history and purpose completely skewed.

The second reason why I chose to research the Panthers is that I respect the attention given by the Panthers to the previously neglected lower income groups. Despite all of its great accomplishments, including the Civil Rights Act of 1964 and Voting Rights Act of 1965, the mainstream, middle-class, Civil Rights Movement did not adequately deal with the pressing concerns of the working class and lower income populace. The

Panthers, on the other hand, were an action-based group that focused on providing services to meet the immediate needs of the masses.

I also elected to write about the Panthers because I appreciate their stance on armed self-defense. Arguably, if Andrew Goodman, Michael Schwerner, and James Chaney had been armed, they may not have been dug out of an earthen dam in Mississippi. Charles R. Sims, founder of the Deacons for Defense, echoed a similar sentiment when he stated "I believe that if the Deacons had been organized in 1964, the three civil rights workers that was murdered in Philadelphia, Mississippi might have been living today because we'd have been there to stop it."[29] I do realize, however, that the success of the Civil Rights Movement also depended on martyrs to a degree. The police, dogs, firehoses, enraged racists, and murder that greeted the nonviolent protestors had a pronounced and visceral effect on the American public that generated much needed support for the Movement.

Another motivation for studying the Panthers is because I grew up in Racine, Wisconsin. As a youth, I was subjected to sound bites on the news from local Milwaukee activist, alderman, and founder of the Black Panther Militia, Michael McGee. The local newscasts often aired McGee's most controversial comments on dealing with poverty, crime and drugs. The news frequently focused on McGee's militant threats to clean up the problems in the city, as he vowed that the Black Panther Militia would use guerilla warfare tactics, if necessary.[30] I grew up with a negative image of McGee, and I also naively thought that McGee and his Militia were the same as the Black Panther Party, but that was not the case. In 1993, I started to question the stereotypical view of the Panthers after watching an *Eyes on the Prize* documentary that portrayed the Panthers as a persecuted organization that provided breakfasts to hungry children. After I saw the film I wanted to learn more about this militant group because of these conflicting images. The following semester I wrote a research paper on the community programs of the Black Panther Party. I then wrote a graduate paper and my Master's Thesis on the Party as well. As trite as it may sound, by 1993, I knew I would write a book on the Black Panther Party.

Finally, I, as a white male, chose to write on the Black Panthers because I honestly believe that they were one of the only organizations from the sixties that sincerely believed that ALL people needed to be free from oppression. As Dakin Gentry from the Milwaukee branch noted in 1969, the Party "was involved in a revolution for all oppressed people, regardless of race."[31]

Other organizations and groups from the same era tended to restrict their focus to only one particular group of oppressed people, often times, to the exclusion of other suppressed groups. For instance, the National Association for the Advancement of Colored People (NAACP) only seemed concerned with middle-class African Americans, while the Nation of Islam focused on lower income and working-class blacks. The post-1966 SNCC concerned themselves with issues affecting African Americans, while the Students for a Democratic Society (SDS) targeted middle-class, white students. The National Organization for Women (NOW) almost exclusively catered to white, middle-class women. And the Brown Berets mainly dealt with issues effecting lower income and working-class Chicanos, while the American Indian Movement (AIM) addressed the concerns of lower income and working-class Native Americans.

The Panthers realized that the struggle went beyond racial, ethnic, and gender lines. For instance, the Panthers embraced coalitions with white, Latino, and Native American groups. In fact, there was a sizable degree of friction between the Panthers and other Black Power groups like SNCC because, by 1967, SNCC preferred not to work with whites.[32] Todd Gitlin, from Students for a Democratic Society (SDS), noted the difference between the Panthers and other Black Power groups when he stated, "At a time when most other black militants donned dashikis and glowered at whites, they (the Panthers) welcomed whites."[33]

Further illustrating the Panthers' belief in the freedom of all people is, is that unlike many other Black Power groups, Panther women played crucial roles within the Party. Some portray Black Power groups as sexist organizations that looked at black male liberation as separate and paramount to that of black female liberation. A prime example of a stereotypically sexist Black Power group is Maulana Karenga's cultural nationalist "Us" organization, founded in Los Angeles in 1965. Black Panther scholar Tracye Matthews writes that Us had "unapologetic male supremacist policies."[34] Karenga himself stated, "We (Us) say Male supremacy is based on three things: tradition, acceptance and reason."[35] A number of Panther women originally were members of Karenga's organization, only to leave after becoming dissatisfied with the discriminatory nature of the group. For example, future Panther Angela Davis noted that while she was a member of Us, she was, "criticized very heavily, especially by male members of Karenga's organization, for doing 'a man's job.' Women should not play leadership roles, they insisted. A woman was supposed to 'inspire' her man and educate his children."[36] Panther leader Elaine Brown also was involved with Us initially, until she realized how blatantly sexist it was. Brown stated that Karenga "raised the name of Africa to justify the suppression of black women."[37]

The Party was vastly different from groups such as Us, evidenced by the large number of women who rose to positions of power within the

Party. For instance, Elaine Brown headed the Black Panthers from 1974-1977. During Brown's time as chairperson of the Party, Ericka Huggins, Phyllis Jackson, Joan Kelley and Norma Armour were all appointed to the ten-member Central Committee; the Panther's main governing body.[38]

The aforementioned Ericka Huggins was another top-ranking Panther. Huggins helped form the New Haven branch of the Party in late 1969, and she served as the Director of the Youth Communal Institute (a fully accredited Panther-operated elementary school), in the Oakland area in 1974.[39] Kathleen Cleaver and Angela Davis also played important roles in the Black Panther Party. Cleaver was a member of the Party's Central Committee during its early years, and Davis helped to galvanize support for the Panthers as a result of her highly publicized flight for freedom. Connie Matthews, a highly respected Panther ambassador, represented the Party abroad in such countries as Sweden, Finland and Norway.[40]

In addition to these relatively well-known Panther women, there were a number of other Panther women who held influential positions within the Party. Yvonne King managed and directed over 500 members as Deputy Minister of Labor for the Illinois chapter. JoNina Abron was the last editor of the Panther's main news source, the *Black Panther*. Irene Simmons was a leading member of the Chattanooga branch of the Party, and Audrea Jones was the Captain of the Boston branch. As Tracye Matthews noted, "Black women were critical players in the Black Panther Party."[41]

The *Black Panther* also helps to show the Party's inclusive nature in terms of gender, by showing countless images and articles about black women. *The Black Panther* clearly illustrates that women were just as integral to the struggle as men. The newspaper did not restrict its coverage of women to Black Panther members either, as there were numerous stories and pictures devoted to women in freedom struggles throughout the globe. For instance, articles in the *Black Panther* told of American Indian women who had been illegally sterilized in Oklahoma, and of women who demonstrated for better working conditions in Ethiopia. The Party gave front-page attention to International Women's Day, and there was a whole series of articles that addressed the rampant sexism and racism faced by black women in the United States' Armed Forces.[42]

The Black Panthers, however, were by no means a gender-neutral group without sexist members or policies. Many stories have been told by Panthers about how male Black Panthers tried to use their rank to force female Panthers to have sex with them. A former Black Panther, Earl Anthony, reportedly told Elaine Brown that a "true sister would be happy to sleep with a revolutionary brother."[43] Some Panther women also were relegated to stereotypical "women's jobs," such as office work or cooking.

Sexism within the Party actually caused a number of Panther women, such as Regina Jennings of the Oakland branch, to leave the Party.[44]

Despite the shortcomings of the Party in regard to gender issues, Panther leaders and members did make a serious effort to address sexism within its ranks. For example, a number of branches, such as Milwaukee, suspended or expelled a number of members for sexist behavior.[45] And as Tracye Matthews noted:

> Despite their limitations (or perhaps because of them) and the generally dire circumstances in which they found themselves, the Black Panther Party was still often ahead of most other Black nationalist organizations and many white leftist and mainstream organizations in their progress on addressing (at least rhetorically) 'the woman question.'[46]

In addition to the Party's stance on women and whites, the Panthers also spoke out on behalf of gay organizations at a time when few did so. Furthermore, the Party stood behind various labor unions, and the Panthers supported freedom movements worldwide, ranging from Vietnam to Angola to Ireland.[47]

Since the community programs of the Black Panther Party are most neglected by previous works dealing with the Party, I have specifically targeted this area for in-depth analysis. Other studies of the Panthers were too enamored with sensationalistic events. I have also chosen to focus on the Party from 1966 to 1977, even though the Party as a whole survived until 1982. I chose these years because, as former Black Panther Michael Fultz states, the Party became "non-functional" by 1977. National membership sunk to roughly 100 because of years of political persecution and internal dissension, and the only active Black Panther chapters left were in California.[48]

Furthermore, I decided to focus on Milwaukee because little has been written about the Milwaukee branch of the Black Panther Party. One plausible explanation for the neglect is that nearby Chicago had such a dynamic leader in Fred Hampton. Hampton was a magnetic visionary whose charisma and oratory easily drew members and attention to Chicago. Also, the Chicago branch received even greater national and local publicity when Hampton was tragically murdered, thus inadvertently helping overshadow the rich history of the Milwaukee branch of the Party.

The first chapter of this book attempts to place the Panthers in an historical context in order to illustrate that they were not a complete anomaly in the tradition of African American protest. It is imperative that any contemporary study of the Black Panthers, or any other Black Power group, conceptualizes the Panthers as part of the larger African American struggle for freedom and equality. By approaching the topic in this fashion, it will be easier to think of the Panthers as part of a rich African American tradition of armed resistance as well as practitioners of community service. If the Black Panther Party is not analyzed in such a fashion, it then becomes much easier for critics to dismiss the organization as a rogue band of extremists who were not representative of the needs of a large percentage of African Americans.

The second chapter examines the specifics of the Black Panther Party, especially the community programs on a national scale, in order for the reader to better understand the Party and its community programs were not isolated occurrences. Chapter two also includes other important information, such as how the Panthers specifically funded their programs. In addition, chapter two explores how the Panther programs were received by the larger African American community, and where the programs tended to be located.

The following chapters form a case study of the Milwaukee branch of the Black Panther Party. Chapter three addresses the conditions of lower income and working-class black Milwaukee, with the hope of illustrating how and why the Panthers came into existence in the city. Chapter three also analyzes the rich history of African American protest in Milwaukee in order to contextualize the Panthers. Furthermore, this chapter also provides background information about former Mayor Henry Maier, and former Chief of Police Harold Breier, because they played such powerful roles in Milwaukee in the 1960s and 1970s.

Chapter four covers the many different community programs of the Milwaukee Black Panthers, in order to show their deep commitment to providing for the community. And Chapter five highlights the very successful Breakfast for Children Program in Milwaukee, which ultimately paved the way for the Hunger Task Force, the largest food pantry in Milwaukee, and for the Milwaukee School District's Breakfast Program.

Chapter six shows some of the flaws and problems that plagued the Party. I believe this chapter is necessary because it demonstrates that the Party had failings. I will argue, however, that whatever its mistakes in style and tactics, the Black Panther Party should be viewed as an organization with a clear desire to improve the economic, social and political conditions of lower income and working-class African Americans. The Panthers were not racists, crooks, or opportunists, although there were some such individuals in their ranks. The accomplishments and worth of an organization, however, cannot be judged by the actions of a handful of individuals. If this were the case, then members of the Democratic Party would be characterized as marital infidels, thanks to Bill Clinton, and the members of the Republican Party would be labeled as members of the White Citizen's Council, thanks to Trent Lott. As laughable as these statements may seem, it has been with such caricatures and shallow analysis that the history of the Black Panther Party has been written by many scholars, journalists, and filmmakers. Any organization must be viewed by the words and actions of the majority of its members, and what the majority of Black Panthers wanted was, "Power to all people," not "power over people."[49]

My conclusion briefly compares and contrasts the Milwaukee branch with other Panther branches so that I can re-assert that the Milwaukee branch was not an isolated phenomenon. I also include a number of appendices in my dissertation that will cover such items as The Ten-Point Program of the Panthers, members of the Milwaukee Black Panther Party and which Panther branches had various community programs.

The bulk of the information for *The Black Panthers in the Midwest* comes from primary sources, such as the *Milwaukee Courier*, *The Black Panther*, the Social Action Vertical File at the Wisconsin State Historical Society, and the University of Wisconsin-Milwaukee Archives. I recognize that extensive use of newspapers can present various shortcomings, as often times, the stories may be biased in one direction or another, and that could lead to incorrect assessments. For instance, the mainstream presses in Milwaukee, the *Journal* and the *Sentinel*, were fairly conservative, whereas the black newspapers in Milwaukee, the *Courier* and the *Greater Milwaukee Star*, were much more liberal. The use of oral testimonies presents additional difficulties in evaluating the information. Certain individuals may have an objective they want to accomplish in their interview, or maybe they have forgotten events or details from the past. In addition, I do wish that I had collected more oral histories from former Black Panthers as part of this work, but a handful of individuals would not talk to me about their past experiences for various reasons, and a number of others could not be located. Nevertheless, by corroborating material gathered from newspapers and interviews with data from countless other sources, I believe I offer as thorough and accurate of an assessment of the Black Panther Party as possible.

In closing, I also wanted to include more FBI records in this work, but it took the FBI roughly two years to answer my Freedom of Information Act request. Furthermore, the FBI only sent me records from January through August of 1969, even though I requested information through 1977. The FBI stated that they sent me a partial shipment so as "to avoid further delays." Good thing the FBI has a sense of humor.

Chapter One
Picking up the Gun and Serving the People

Any contemporary study of the Black Panthers, or any other Black Power group, must place them in the context of the larger African American struggle for freedom and equality, as well as evaluate their historical significance in terms of mainstream American history. So doing will make it easier to conceptualize the Panthers as part of a rich African American tradition of armed resistance and community service.

The history of African American armed self-defense runs very deep, going back to the antebellum period, in fact. For instance, the legendary Harriet Tubman always carried a gun while spiriting ex-slaves to freedom on the Underground Railroad during the 1850s. Tubman was not going to suffer herself, or any of her "passengers," to be harmed or returned to slavery.[1] Another early example is the infamous New York City draft riot in July of 1863. The riot occurred after President Lincoln had issued the Emancipation Proclamation, leading many whites to perceive that the war aims had changed, and that they were being drafted in order to free the slaves, as opposed to preserving the Union. Roughly a dozen blacks were killed in this atrocity as white rioters displaced their anger at the draft and the Emancipation Proclamation, on to the local African American population. Despite the grave risks, many African Americans in New York chose to defend their communities rather than flee. For instance, "In Weeksville and Flatbush (New York City neighborhoods) the colored men who had manhood in them armed themselves . . . determined to die defending their homes." And, "Most of the colored men in Brooklyn who remained in the city were armed for self-defense."[2]

The pattern of armed resistance continued through Reconstruction, as throngs of southern blacks, especially Civil War veterans, became involved in "militias." Towards the end of Reconstruction, states such as Mississippi and Louisiana witnessed the Ku Klux Klan and other racist groups systematically killing and terrorizing blacks in the name of white supremacy. African Americans knew they had to protect their own communities because the federal government became less and less concerned with the plight of blacks. Out of this climate, the militias were born with the purpose of defending African American communities and preserving the right to vote. Black militias conducted parades and drills similar to military regiments, taking a calculated risk to test the theory that a show of black militancy would serve as a deterrent to white violence. Militias fought numerous gun battles with white aggressors, and the outnumbered African Americans more than held their own in most instances. According to historian Robert Cruden, "Many militia companies fought stubbornly when attacked."[3] Noted scholar Herbert Shapiro states that "where offered the opportunity blacks readily volunteered to join the militia and fought back when attacked by racists."[4] Shapiro goes on to write that in November of 1874, in Charleston, South Carolina, that "whites began the violence but more than met their match" from the local black militia.[5] The Black Panther Party of the 1960s and 1970s strongly resembled the militias of the 1860s and 1870s. Both groups were armed and practiced self-defense, obviously, but they also took great pride in their display of strength before white vigilantes.

Many historians refer to 1880–1915 as the nadir, or lowest point, of race relations in this country. These years were plagued by a huge rise in lynchings, and in the formal establishment of legalized segregation throughout the South, as white southerners sought to consolidate power in a post-Reconstruction era South.[6] Nevertheless, African Americans practiced armed self-defense during the Nadir. One such example of armed resistance during the Nadir, occurred in March 1892 in Memphis, Tennessee, when three African American storeowners were forced to pick up arms to defend themselves and their livelihood.

Thomas Moss, Calvin McDowell, and Henry Stewart owned a store that was located directly across the street from a white-owned store, and the white proprietors did not appreciate the business competition. Therefore, one night a white mob led by the white proprietors, attempted to burn down the store of the three African Americans. Moss, McDowell, and Stewart, armed with shotguns and rifles, temporarily held off a white mob, wounding three whites in the process. Despite the heroics of the three African Americans, they were eventually lynched for wounding the three whites. Nevertheless, the actions of Moss, McDowell, and Stewart are a testament to the presence of armed self-defense in African American communities.[7]

The lynching of the aforementioned black entrepreneurs enraged Ida B. Wells, a Memphis resident, who was a friend of the three men. Wells became a famous anti-lynching spokesperson largely as a result of these lynchings. A lesser known fact about Wells, however, is that she firmly believed in armed resistance as well. As scholar Paula Giddings writes:

> Ida B. Wells didn't believe in the ultimate efficacy of passive resistance, however. She purchased a pistol, determined to 'sell my life as dearly as possible,' and suggested that other Blacks do the same. 'A Winchester rifle should have a place of honor in every home,' Wells told her community. 'When the white man . . . knows he runs as great a risk of biting the dust every time his Afro-American victim does, he will have greater respect for Afro-American life.[8]

The pattern of armed resistance on the part of African Americans continued through the early 1900s, evidenced by the Atlanta riot of 1906. Herbert Shapiro notes that, "When police opened fire upon a group of blacks on the street the blacks responded in kind, and one officer was killed and another wounded."[9] While teaching at Atlanta University during this chaotic era, the renowned W.E.B DuBois also urged African Americans in Atlanta to use armed resistance to defend themselves and their communities. DuBois proclaimed that "effective guns in the hands of black people determined to sell their souls dearly" would prevent whites from committing acts of violence on the black populace.[10] DuBois, therefore, bought a shotgun and 2,000 rounds of ammunition to protect himself and his community. If any whites sought to inflict violence on DuBois, he would "spray their guts over the grass."[11]

Elaine, Arkansas in 1919 provides yet another illustration of armed self-defense. In early October of that year, black farmers in the community founded The Organization of the Progressive Farmers' and Household Union of America to protest the unfair settlements they were receiving from the white landowners. They held regularly scheduled meetings to discuss ways of creating a more equitable labor system. These meetings were protected by well-armed guards because of fear of reprisal from the hostile planters. Eventually the planters instigated a battle with the black union members, who fought back fiercely even though the odds were not in their favor.[12]

Rosewood, Florida, an all-black town, made famous by a Hollywood-film, also witnessed armed resistance by African Americans. In 1923, a black convict escaped from a chain-gang near Sumner, Florida. A few days later, a white woman in Sumner claimed she was beaten by a black man, and the white townspeople immediately thought it was the escaped convict. Evidence later revealed that she was beaten by a white man with whom she was having an extramarital affair, but in order to conceal the affair she resorted to the all-too-common accusation that she was assaulted by a black male. As a result, the white community of Sumner went on a rampage against the neighboring black community of Rosewood, completely destroying the town and killing an estimated 40 to 150 African Americans. The white mob did meet staunch resistance during the killing spree. For instance, a local African American named Sylvester Carrier, temporarily held off the mob, killing at least two and wounding several more.[13]

Dr. Ossian Sweet offers another example of African Americans practicing armed self-defense. In 1925, in Detroit, Sweet bought a home in a predominantly white section of town. Shortly thereafter, Sweet's home was stoned, but shots rang out from inside the home, killing one of the members of the white mob. Sweet was arrested for killing the white assailant, but he was later freed after a lengthy trial. What is especially illuminating about the Sweet incident is that it illustrates that middle-class African Americans from the urban north, also practiced armed resistance.[14]

The use of armed self-defense was also evident in the 1930s, once again with southern sharecropping unions. Some members of the unions went on strike to protest their exploitation, provoking planters to respond by intimidating, beating, and killing African Americans who participated in these unions. One such example occurred near Camp Hill, Alabama in 1931. Black sharecroppers held a meeting near Camp Hill, but police raided the party and beat roughly eighty members. The very next day, 150 sharecroppers held another meeting southwest of Camp Hill, in a vacant house, but they posted sentries outside to warn them of possible raids. Once again, the meeting was raided by the local police, but the sharecroppers, led by Ralph Gray, shot at the attackers, killing Sheriff Kyle Young. The sharecroppers retreated to Gray's home, and barricaded themselves inside. The African American sharecroppers fought off the marauding whites long enough so that almost all of the sharecroppers could flee out the back of the house. Gray, however, refused to leave, choosing instead to stay and defend his home. Ultimately, Gray was killed, and his body was unceremoniously dumped on the nearby Dadeville (AL) Courthouse lawn.[15] The Camp Hill incident provides yet another clear illustration of African Americans engaging in armed self-defense, even if the consequence was death.

The Camp Hill affair did not deter local sharecroppers from organizing, it merely strengthened their resolve, and willingness to arm themselves. As a result, future sharecropping meetings in the Dadeville area had what some observers referred to as a "small arsenal" for protection.[16] As Secretary of the Sharecropper's Union, Albert Jackson, noted in 1935, Union members in Alabama were more than willing to defend themselves. Citing the Jim Meriweather incident, Jackson wrote, "The night Jim Meriweather was killed the strikers got their guns and waited for another vigilante attack. When the lynchers arrived the strikers sounded the battle cry, it was to be steel for steel on even terms." Because of the Union's militant actions, the whites left without a shot being fired.[17]

Perhaps the most well-known member of the aforementioned Sharecropper's Union was Nate Shaw. Shaw grew up in Alabama at the turn of the twentieth century, yet he routinely rebelled against the oppressive Southern society in a number of ways. He refused to pay debts he owed to whites who wronged him. Shaw never let whites raise their hand against him or steal property or possessions from other African Americans in the community without a confrontation. More than once, Shaw pulled his gun on whites who threatened him with knives or guns of their own. Inevitably, Shaw was forced into a gunfight with white authorities who shot him in his legs and ultimately sentenced him to twelve years in prison. Shaw stated, "I didn't run nowhere. I stood just like I'm standing today—when I know I'm right and I ain't harmin' nobody and nothin' else, I'll give you trouble if you try to move me." Nate Shaw also proclaimed that, "Somebody got to stand up. If we don't, we niggers in this country are easy prey."[18] Shaw recognized that African Americans in his situation could not afford to be non-violent, something the Panthers would also grasp.

Yet another illustration of armed resistance occurred on February 25, 1946 in Columbia, Tennessee. A white male storeowner had an altercation with a local black woman named Gladys Stephenson, which prompted Gladys's son, James, to throw the storeowner through a window. James was quickly arrested and then released that night on bail, causing some local whites to discuss the necessity of using lynch law to keep blacks in line. A white mob began to gather and they prepared to enter the black community of Columbia, known as Mink Slide. In turn, African Americans living in the Mink Slide district prepared for the white mob. Four Columbia police officers were sent in to Mink Slide supposedly to cool down the black community. It was reported that, "The men (police) had not gone far when they heard shouted orders to halt—and when they didn't comply, shots rang out. All four were wounded, one seriously, and they retreated."[19] Given the historical context of southern police-black community relations, the actions of the Mink Slide residents can be seen as prudent self-defense.

Proponents of armed resistance during the 1940s could be found in traditionally non-violent organizations as well. Even Walter White, the conservative President of the National Association for the Advancement of Colored People (NAACP) during the 1940s, recognized the legitimacy of African Americans engaging in armed resistance.[20]

Despite the fact that the 1950s and 1960s were the peak of the non-violent Civil Rights Movement, there also were countless African Americans who engaged in armed resistance during this time. Many African Americans embraced non-violence during the Civil Rights Movement, but it was not what Martin Luther King termed, a strategy of "pure nonviolence."[21] According to King, "pure nonviolence" required too much self-restraint and discipline for it to be popular with the masses. Non-violent leaders such as King, realized that "The principle of self-defense, even involving weapons and bloodshed, has never been condemned, even by Gandhi."[22] Therefore, the non-violent movement needed to make certain allowances for self-defense, if it hoped to be successful. For example, Reverend William A. Bender, leader of the Tougaloo, Mississippi chapter of the NAACP, an organization that routinely espoused non-violence, kept a .38 revolver on his person during the 1950s.[23] E.W. Steptoe, who organized the Amite County, Mississippi chapter of the NAACP, was an African American farmer who "was legendary for his arsenal."[24]

It was also not just members of the working-class, however, who engaged in armed self-defense, as Emmett Stringer, a dentist, and T.R.M Howard, a doctor, clearly illustrate. Stringer, once the state president of the NAACP in Mississippi, stated, "I had weapons in my house. And not only in my house, I had weapons on me when I went to my office, because I knew people were out to get me."[25] And T.R.M Howard, a prominent African American physician in Mount Bayou, Mississippi, and high-ranking member of the Mississippi NAACP, employed armed bodyguards to guard his house twenty-four hours a day.[26]

Perhaps the most renowned member of the NAACP in the Deep South at this time was Medgar Evers. Evers, leader of the Jackson, Mississippi branch of the NAACP, was another believer in African Americans employing armed resistance. Evers even contemplated the necessity of African Americans participating in a guerilla war in order to thwart further attacks on the black populace.[27]

Armed resistance was also practiced during the legendary Montgomery Bus Boycott of 1955–1956. The Bus Boycott started after an African American woman named Rosa Parks was arrested for refusing to give up her seat to white passengers. As a result, the Boycott's main goal was the desegregation of the buses in Montgomery, with the hope that it would serve as a precedent for future desegregation efforts. The Boycott was led by individuals such as the aforementioned Parks, and E.D. Nixon of the local NAACP, JoAnne Robinson of the Women's Political Council, as well as a very young Martin Luther King, Jr. Despite King's firm belief in conducting a non-violent movement, some African Americans, such as Richmond Smiley, armed themselves in order to protect themselves and King. The presence of armed self-defense in the Boycott was most evident in the wake of the bombing of King's home. After King's home was bombed, dozens of armed African Americans converged on the home to prevent any further attacks. Even more revealing, was when Bayard Rustin, a prominent pacifist and Civil Rights activist, visited King's house, and almost sat on a gun.[28]

The most vigorous individual proponent of armed self-defense during the Civil Rights Movement was Robert Franklin Williams. Williams was an ex-Marine and World War II veteran who returned to his hometown of Monroe, North Carolina in 1955 to find a community bursting at the seams with racial animosity. Whites in Monroe systematically denied blacks the most basic political, social, and educational opportunities. There were also many documented cases of violence directed at the African American citizens of Monroe.[29] Like many African American veterans, Williams could not reconcile defending a country in the name of democracy that did not grant him the most fundamental human rights. Serving in the military instilled a sizable degree of militancy in Williams and other black veterans.[30] Williams could not sit idly by and watch his community being terrorized, so he and other military veterans in the vicinity organized a new and improved NAACP chapter in Monroe. The previous chapter had dissolved due to lack of support, but not before making Williams its leader. Even though Williams' organization was an NAACP chapter, it bore few similarities to other branches of the NAACP, which were primarily middle-class. The Monroe branch was made up primarily of members of lower income groups and the working classes, who strongly believed in the armed defense of black communities.[31]

Williams fervently believed in the necessity for self-defense, not in aggressive violence.[32] Williams did not advocate violence against whites, although many scholars argue otherwise. The main reason for this misperception of Williams was his militant stance as well as one particular emotional outburst. In 1959, when a "not guilty" verdict was issued in favor of two white men who raped a black woman in North Carolina, the African American women in the courtroom verbally attacked Williams for not adequately defending them.[33] In a natural bout of anger and frustration, Williams reacted by vowing to "meet violence with violence."[34] Regardless of Williams' firm commitment to the principles of self-defense, this one verbal mistake caused him to lose his position in the NAACP and indelibly and inaccurately labeled him as a supporter of violence. August Meier and Elliot Rudwick, renowned for their dispassionate scholarship, are among those scholars who have characterized Williams as calling for "open advocacy of violence against the oppressive white community," yet nothing was further from the truth.[35]

Gloria House states in the Introduction to a reprint of Williams' *Negroes With Guns*, "First it is important to be clear that Williams advocated self-defense, not aggression."[36] Williams, himself, stated, "I wish to make it clear that I do not advocate violence for its own sake or for the sake of reprisals against whites."[37] The first chapter of *Negroes with Guns* is fittingly entitled, "Self-Defense Prevents Bloodshed."[38] Williams routinely maintained that if African Americans did not defend themselves, they would continually be subjected to violence.[39]

Williams also gives credence to the claim that self-defense is not an aberration in African American history. Williams writes, "We know that the average Afro-American is not a pacifist. He is not a pacifist and he has never been a pacifist and he is not made of the type of material that would make a good pacifist."[40] Historian Tim Tyson makes the legitimate claim that, "It might be argued that nonviolent interracialism rather than Black Power, is the anomaly in American history." Furthermore, Tyson states that, "Our vision of the African American freedom movement between 1945 and 1965 as characterized solely and inevitably by nonviolent civil rights protest obscures the full complexity of racial politics."[41] Tyson goes on to note that Williams's "defiance—and that of thousands of other black activists— testifies to the fact that throughout the 'Civil Rights' era, black Southerners stood prepared to defend home and family by force."[42] Further illustrating Tyson's point, Roy Wilkins, the head of the NAACP in the 1950s, and the individual responsible for ousting Williams from the NAACP, stated, "Like Williams I believe in self-defense. While I admire Reverend King's theories of overwhelming enemies with love, I don't think I could have put those theories into practice myself."[43]

Armed resistance on the part of African Americans continued throughout the 1960s. For instance, on May 14, 1961, Fred Shuttlesworth from the Southern Christian Leadership Conference (SCLC), led an armed fifteen-car caravan from Birmingham to Anniston, Alabama to safely transport Freedom Riders whose bus was set ablaze. Also in 1961, Ralph Abernathy of SCLC, had his Montgomery church besieged by whites during a Civil Rights gathering. Black men in the church retrieved guns and knives from their coats and, "There were heated whispers in the wings as some of them told the preachers that they were not about to let the mob burn or bludgeon their families without a fight, even in church."[44] Apparently the "turn-the-other-cheek" philosophy was not completely embraced by all, even those who were sympathetic towards the teachings of Martin Luther King, Jr. and the SCLC.

While a number of urban southern African Americans practiced armed self-defense, there were many more rural dwelling African Americans in the South who embraced armed resistance as a way of life. As Civil Rights historian, Clayborne Carson notes, there was a "long-standing tradition of armed self-defense among blacks in the rural deep South."[45] One such example is Hartman Turnbow from Holmes County, Mississippi. Turnbow was a follower of Martin Luther King, Jr.'s teachings, but just in case, he kept a Remington twelve-gauge in his house and an automatic pistol in a briefcase that he always carried. As Civil Rights scholar Taylor Branch, notes, "SNCC workers cheerfully overlooked the arsenal of firearms that he (Turnbow) had concealed in at least a dozen places on his property and person."[46] Turnbow was not the exception either. Julian Bond, a high-ranking member of SNCC, stated "Almost everybody with whom we stayed in Mississippi, had guns, as a matter of course, hunting guns. But you know, they were there for other purposes too." [47] Even though there were numerous instances of violence directed against SNCC workers in the deep South, it would have been much worse had it not been for individuals like Turnbow. As Clayborne Carson states, "The relative paucity of violence in some communities was attributed by SNCC workers not to the federal presence but to the willingness of blacks to arm themselves."[48]

C.O. Chinn, of Madison County, Mississippi, was very similar to Turnbow. Chinn worked with the Congress of Racial Equality (CORE), in the early 1960s, but despite CORE's commitment to non-violence, Chinn kept a weapon openly displayed on the front seat of his car. As a result, according to CORE activist Matt Suarez, "Every white man in the town knew that you didn't fuck with C.O. Chinn."[49]

In addition, African American males were not the only ones willing to pick up arms in the name of self-defense. NAACP activists, C.C. Bryant and his wife Ora, of McComb County, Mississippi, defended their home together from non-stop attacks by white nightriders during the mid-1960s. When their home was bombed on one particular occasion in 1964, both C.C. and Ora fired upon the white criminals. Afterwards, C.C. and Ora "took turns standing guard over their house every night, a pattern that became standard procedure in black McComb."[50]

Laura McGee, a local activist of Greenwood, Mississippi, also did not sit back idly when faced with threats of violence. After white hoodlums fired into her home in July of 1964, she called the sheriff and told him he needed to stop such attacks, because if he did not, he was going to "be picking up bodies (of the attackers) the next time she called."[51] Even Daisy Bates, who ridiculed the militant Robert F. Williams for being a proponent of armed self-defense, kept her gun, "Old-Betsy' well-oiled" in case of nightrider attacks. In addition, Bates employed armed security guards to protect her house from attacks by whites.[52]

Perhaps one of the most tragically ironic examples of armed self-defense was in the wake of the disappearance of Civil Rights workers Michael Schwerner, Andrew Goodman, and James Cheney in 1964 in Neshoba County, Mississippi. As soon as it became apparent that the three were missing, and probably dead, African Americans from Neshoba went looking for their bodies. While doing so, they were armed as they were determined not to suffer the same fate as Schwerner, Goodman, and Cheney.[53]

African Americans practiced armed self-defense outside the Magnolia state as well. For instance, SNCC members noted that, "Like the rural areas of Mississippi, black farmers in Lowndes County (Alabama) owned weapons and were willing to defend themselves when attacked."[54] Illustrating how deeply imbedded the concept of armed self-defense was in rural African American communities in the rural South at this time, Civil Rights activist Bernard Lafayette held a number of meetings simply to convince black farmers living near Selma, Alabama, to go into town without their rifles.[55]

Armed resistance was found in black communities outside the traditional deep South as well. For example, Robert Hayling, the advisor to the St. Augustine, Florida chapter of the Youth Council of the NAACP, stated in 1963, that, "I and others have armed and we will shoot first and ask questions later. We are not going to die like Medgar Evers."[56] Therefore, after countless car raids by the Klan into the African American section of St. Augustine, during which Klan members fired shotguns into the homes of blacks, one white teenager was killed by return fire, and the car raids stopped.[57]

There are many other examples of African Americans advocating or practicing armed self-defense. Malcolm X called for mobile rifle clubs to defend the lives and homes of black Americans.[58] Malcolm even told Martin Luther King, Jr. in 1964, that all King had to do was "say the word and we will immediately dispatch some of our brothers there (in the South) to organize self-defense units among our people, and the Ku Klux Klan will then receive a taste of its own medicine."[59] As a result of Malcolm's militant ideology and status as a martyr, he would always occupy a place of reverence among the Black Panthers.

Another clear example of African Americans engaging in armed self-defense was the para-police organization known as the Deacons for Defense. The Deacons were initially formed in 1964 in Jonesboro, Louisiana in response to a locally powerful Ku Klux Klan. The Deacons began as a fairly low-key organization with only handfuls of members. By 1966, the Deacons had twenty-one chapters, primarily in Louisiana and Mississippi, and several hundred members, who paid ten dollars to join, and two dollars a month in membership dues.[60] Charles R. Sims, of the Deacons for Defense, stated that the Deacons armed themselves "because we got tired of the women, the children, being harassed by white night-riders."[61] Sims, a World War II veteran, even claimed that his organization was better armed than his hometown police department of Bogalusa, Louisiana. Cleveland Sellers from SNCC reported that "everyone realized that without them (Deacons), our lives would have been much less secure."[62] Much like Robert Williams, the Deacons armed themselves to prevent violence, not to engage in it.[63] An internal memo from the FBI solidified this point, when it noted that the Deacons would not start any conflict, but would counter any violence directed at the black community.[64] Historian Lance Hill also notes that the Deacons were not the first, nor the only African Americans, to engage in armed resistance during the Civil Rights Movement.[65] As Hill states,

> Much of the popular history of the civil rights era rests on the myth of nonviolence: the perception that the movement achieved its goals through nonviolent direct action . . . In this narrative Martin Luther King, Jr. serves as the 'moral metaphor' of the age while black militants—advocates of racial pride and coercive force—are dismissed as ineffective rebels who alienated whites with Black Power rhetoric and violence.[66]

African Americans who engaged in armed self-defense may have alienated the support of white "liberals" and moderates, but more importantly, they tried to protect their basic right to live.

These selected examples illustrate that the Black Panthers were not an isolated phenomenon and they were not simply the product of frustration, as scholars such as August Meier and Elliott Rudwick have suggested.[67] African Americans have engaged in armed resistance in the United States for hundreds of years, and understandably so. As long as blacks are subjected to acts of racial violence, there will be a segment of the black populace that is willing to defend themselves.

In addition to providing the community service of armed-defense, the Black Panthers also had a strong commitment to providing material goods for poor African Americans, not unlike Daddy Grace, Father D⸱⸱⸱ne, the Garvey Movement and the Nation of Islam. These individuals / ments clearly show a pattern of African Americans providing fortunate members of their communities.

Marcus Garvey's Universal Negro Improvement Association (UNIA) of the early 1920's, is illustrative of the community-help mentality that has been an important part of numerous black movements. One of the most pressing goals of the UNIA, was "to administer to and assist the needy."[68] Garvey proclaimed that "there should be an equitable distribution and apportionment of all such things." Garveyites provided food, clothing, health care and temporary sleeping quarters to indigent African Americans.[69] The social services of the UNIA greatly diminished after Garvey was deported to Jamaica in 1925 for committing mail fraud.

Daddy Grace was one of many Harlem preachers during the Depression who sought to provide social services to the community. Grace established a pension fund for his old and poor members. He also gave away free food, clothing, and provided shelter during emergencies, and he ran a number of low-priced laundries, barber shops, and restaurants.[70] Even though Grace provided for his community, his humanitarian efforts never came close to matching those of the legendary Father Divine.

Father Divine was an active Harlem preacher in the 1930s who was recognized by his followers as a savior. Some Divine supporters declared that "Father Divine is God!"[71] Divine was a hands-on religious figure who felt the pressing need to take care of the poor in the world. He owned a restaurant in Harlem where he fed the poor at subsidized rates. It was reported that fifty cents bought four plates of food, or enough to feed a moderately-sized family. Claude McKay surveyed a Divine establishment and found that, "The food is good and plentiful. A good piece of meat and two vegetables cost ten cents; a piece of cake or ice-cream, five cents; coffee or soft drinks, three cents."[72] Divine meals consisted of fricasseed chicken, roast duck, spareribs, ice cream and chocolate cake. Robert Weisbrot writes, "Observers marveled at the opulence of the meals which impressed even for prosperous times."[73] A reported 2,500–3,000 people were fed daily at Divine restaurants.[74] Father Divine also provided clothing, coal, jobs and housing for the poor. The destitute were housed in "Divine Hotels" for a miniscule charge. Sara Harris claims that people could stay in the Divine Riviera in Newark or the Divine Tracy in Philadelphia for two dollars a week. Divine also had six, four-story houses on 126th and Lennox in Harlem that housed 300 people at a dollar a week.[75] Author Jill Watts reports that "Father Divine provided anyone who lived on a marginal income . . . with much needed social assistance."[76] Watts also states that Divine donated food and shelter to impoverished blacks, and that he operated a free employment agency for those in need of work.[77]

Reminiscent of Garvey's UNIA, the Nation of Islam, founded by W.D. Fard in Detroit in 1931, also had a measurable component of self-help in their organization. One of the most successful community services provided by the Nation was their six-stage drug rehabilitation program. Unlike expensive treatment centers, the Nation's drug-rehab system was free to its members.[78]

The Panther's community efforts also followed in a long pattern of self-help that was present in many African American communities. Viewing the Panthers in this historical light, it becomes impossible to cast them as either the product of frustration, or as "a temporary media phenomenon," as anti-Panther journalist, Hugh Pearson, argues.[79] The Panthers attempted to meet the pressing needs of lower and working-class African Americans in a variety of ways, and it is time that historians look beyond the misunderstood political surface in assessing the legacy of the Panthers.

Chapter Two
To Serve and Protect

During the 1960s and early 1970s, the United States witnessed massive social unrest throughout the nation. As a result of America's involvement in Vietnam, a strong Anti-War Movement emerged throughout the nation, primarily on college campuses. The Counterculture Movement also blossomed during this time, as throngs of Americans rejected what they perceived to be the failings of American society, evidenced by the war in Vietnam, and rampant racism and poverty in the United States. In addition, the Women's Movement, Gay Liberation Movement, as well as Chicano, Asian American and Native American Movements all came of age during this time, as numerous oppressed groups stood up for their rights. The brunt of the dissension, however, largely stemmed from the centuries of oppression that African Americans were forced to endure.

Many white and black Americans united in the non-violent Civil Rights Movement, struggling to guarantee African Americans their basic human rights. The mainstream Movement was led by individuals such as Martin Luther King, Jr. and Roy Wilkins and their philosophies of non-violence. Advocates of non-violent tactics believed that this strategy was the best vehicle to expose the brutality of the oppressor.[1] Some blacks and whites realized that the philosophies of non-violence were not realistic, given the society in which they were forced to live. George Jackson, who was drafted into the Panther Party wrote:

> The [Martin Luther] Kings, [Roy] Wilikinses, and [Whitney] Youngs exhort us in King's words to 'put away your knives, put away your arms and clothe yourselves in the breastplate of righteousness' and 'turn the other cheek to prove our capacity to endure, to love.' Well, that is good for them perhaps, but I most certainly need both sides of my head.[2]

Another former Panther, Angela Davis, was attracted to the Party because it stated that it would no longer tolerate police brutality in its neighborhoods, and that the Panthers would defend these communities.[3] Revolutionaries such as Davis did not turn to the teachings of Mahatma Ghandi for their ideology, as King had done. Instead, they focused on works like Frantz Fanon's *Wretched of the Earth* and Robert William's *Negroes With Guns*. Fanon's work documents the struggles of a colonized people in Algeria and how they eventually overthrew the oppressive French colonists. Some African Americans, such as Panther co-founders Huey Newton and Bobby Seale, easily saw the parallels between the French and American governments. Also, the Panthers grasped the importance of the "lumpenproletariat," a Marxist term used to refer to the lower-class masses. According to Fanon, these masses should decide what is best for a nation because they represented the nation more accurately than other groups.[4]

Bobby Seale acknowledged that the Panthers respected the philosophy of non-violence, but he argued that it was more practical for people to defend themselves and their community than to engage in sit-ins and marches.[5] Similar sentiments were echoed by some newspapers, which ridiculed the countless Civil Rights marches that seemed not to have any tangible results for many African Americans. Headlines such as, "The March Went on and on and on and got the Black Man Nowhere" became a more frequent complaint among newspaper columnists.[6] Author Roy E. Finkenbine states, "The boycotts, marches, sit-ins, and freedom rides had raised black awareness and expectations but could do little to ameliorate the conditions of ghetto life."[7] Noted Black Panther Party scholars, Charles E. Jones and Judson L. Jeffries, strengthen this claim, when they write that the Civil Rights Movement did little to change the "life chances of African American people."[8] The traditional Civil Rights Movement had come and gone, and in 1969, thirty-two percent of African Americans still made less than $3,000 a year, as compared to only thirteen percent of whites earning the same amount or less. Median annual income for blacks was $4,481, while whites averaged $7,517 a year.[9]

The dissatisfaction with the results of the conventional Civil Rights Movement helped lead to the emergence of a strong Black Power Movement in the mid-1960s. It was in this context that the Black Panther Party was formed in Oakland, California in October of 1966, by Huey Newton and Bobby Seale. Like other Black Power advocates, the Party emphasized the need for African American political and economic empowerment, development of cultural pride, and the right to self-defense.[10] Newton and Seale recognized that large numbers of black Americans were forced to live in intolerable conditions, and they needed immediate and tangible help.[11]

Poverty, inadequate education and health care, and police brutality were all grave problems facing many black communities. The Kerner Commission of 1968 concurred with the Panther co-founders when it noted that segregation and poverty had created a "destructive environment" for many African Americans.[12]

The Party set out to address the various problems affecting lower-income African American communities with a ten-point program which called for decent housing, greater educational opportunities and an end to police brutality (see Appendix A). The Party also advocated that African Americans should arm themselves, so that whites, most specifically the police, would not be able to commit further atrocities upon blacks. By the early 1970s, the Black Panther Party had established over thirty branches in twenty-five cities in the United States and membership reached roughly 3,500 members. The Panthers eventually spread outside the United States to Israel, England and France.[13]

Even though the Panthers won some support across the nation and throughout the world, they never received widespread acceptance because most whites, as well as a sizable percentage of blacks, could not get past the guns and militant rhetoric of the Panthers. As Huey Newton stated, "Our ten-point program was ignored and our plans for survival overlooked. The Black Panthers were identified with the gun."[14] Newspaper reports about the Panthers focused almost exclusively on the militant aspect of the Panthers. The rest of the media were exclusively preoccupied with the Panthers' weaponry, not their ideology or community programs.[15] Black Power scholar, William Van Deburg, solidified this point when he noted that the media was exclusively concerned with the Panthers' weaponry.[16]

The Federal government was also preoccupied with the confrontational tactics of the Panthers. In 1969, the head of the Federal Bureau of Investigation (FBI), J. Edgar Hoover, went so far as to warn that the Black Panthers were the number one internal threat to national security. As a result of Hoover's obsessive concerns, the FBI proceeded to make life very difficult for the Black Panther Party, something that records from the FBI clearly illustrate.[17]

For instance, the FBI routinely informed the nation that the Panthers wanted to overthrow the United States' Government and start "a war of liberation." The Federal Government believed that if the Panthers were portrayed as "authentic gangsters," no one would pay attention to their social programs or political demands.[18] The FBI also issued internal memos that demanded the implementation of "imaginative and hard-hitting counterintelligence measures aimed at crippling the Black Panther Party."[19] In response to memos such as this, the FBI used their Counter Intelligence Program (COINTELPRO) to greatly disrupt the activities of the Panthers.

COINTELPRO was established in the late 1950s, at the height of the Cold War and it initially targeted groups and individuals with supposed Communist affiliations. By 1960, Hoover used COINTELPRO to investigate any group or individual, such as SDS or Martin Luther King, Jr., that demanded social change. Then, in 1968, COINTELPRO turned its attention towards the Black Panthers. COINTELPRO used many devious methods to sabotage the Black Panther Party.[20] For instance, by 1969, it was estimated that the Federal government had sixty to seventy paid informers within the Party.[21] And according to scholars Ward Churchill and Jim Vander Wall, "There can be little doubt that political assassination was a weapon in the COINTELPRO arsenal."[22]

In addition, the FBI exacerbated tensions between the political-oriented Black Panthers and other radical groups, such as Maulana Karenga's Los Angeles-based cultural nationalist organization, "Us" (as opposed to "them"). The existing animosity between Us and the Panthers largely stemmed from their differing ideological stances. The Panthers emphasized political and economic change, whereas Us wanted African Americans to exclusively focus on becoming proud of their heritage and culture. As a result of the differing belief systems, numerous newspaper articles in the *Black Panther* ridiculed cultural nationalists. For instance, an article in the February 2nd, 1969 edition of the *Black Panther*, stated:

> Cultural nationalism manifests itself in many ways but all of these manifestations are essentially grounded in one fact; a universal denial and ignoring of the present political, social, and economic realities and a concentration on the past as a frame of reference.[23]

The FBI took advantage of the precarious situation and mailed derogatory letters to the Panthers that were supposedly from Us, but were actually from FBI agents. Law enforcement agent, Louis E. Tackwood, told Karenga to stop the growth of the Panthers regardless of the consequences. Tackwood informed Karenga "that no 'rangatang'—that's what we called those people—will ever be convicted of murder." Agent Tackwood reported that Karenga was given money and guns from law enforcement officials in order to neutralize the Panthers. Some authors, such as Churchill and Vander Wall, maintain that the FBI congratulated itself for coercing Us to kill two Black Panthers, John Huggins and Alpentice "Bunchy" Carter. Huey Newton stated, "There is no doubt that the Bureau desired violence to occur between the two organizations."[24]

The FBI also mailed fake assassination letters to the leader of Chicago's Blackstone Rangers (a local and powerful gang), Jeff Fort, and signed them with the Panther logo. The Rangers had an estimated 3,000 members, and if they had joined forces with the Chicago branch of the Panthers, the Party would have had a sizable political presence in the Chicago area. The FBI also severely disrupted the already tenuous alliance between the Panthers and the Student Non-violent Coordinating Committee (SNCC), for example, by calling Stokely Carmichael's mother to inform her that the Panthers were going to kill her son.[25]

Local police also helped to destroy the Black Panther Party through harassment, infiltration, entrapment, imprisonment on trumped-up charges, and provoking shoot-outs with the Panthers. Some observers of the period contend that a "genocidal war" was waged on the Black Panther Party, evidenced by the myriad Panther-police shoot-outs.[26] Charles Jones also argues that "Police-Panther gun battles became a defining feature of the early Panther experience," evidenced by the six Panthers who were killed by police in 1969.[27] Others claim that "the police throughout the nation initiated a wave of actual violence against the Panthers, the vehemence of which has not been seen in this country since the attacks on labor at the turn of the century."[28]

Panther Offices in Los Angeles, Oakland, Sacramento, Chicago, and Des Moines were either riddled with bullets or bombed by the police during this era of Panther persecution. To disrupt the activities of Panthers even further, law enforcement officials allegedly stole food and donations from the Breakfast for Children programs in Chicago, Los Angeles, and New York.[29] Huey Newton remarked, "Since its inception, the Party has been subject to a variety of actions by agencies and officers of the federal government intended to destroy it politically and financially."[30] Despite the almost constant harassment by various law enforcement agencies, the Party implemented a number of social welfare programs and community services, called "survival programs" by the Party that illustrated a deep commitment to working-class African American communities.

One of the first issues the Panthers believed they had to address was police brutality. In fact, some scholars have argued that the foremost reason for the existence of the Party was to put an end to the incessant police brutality faced by African Americans.[31] Police brutality was, and still is, a very real threat to many black Americans. One explanation is that the worst police officers are put in crime-infested areas, as a form of punishment. Since these impoverished high-crime areas tend to have a disproportionately high number of African Americans, the dynamic between police and black communities is highly explosive.[32]

Evidence of police brutality was illustrated in the Kerner Commission, which was formed to explain the causes of the widespread rioting between 1966–1967. In its final analysis, the Commission directed a large portion of the blame at police officers. The Kerner Commission stated: "To some Negroes, police have come to symbolize white power, white racism, and white repression." The Commission went on to state, "We have cited deep hostility between police and ghetto communities as a primary cause of the disorders surveyed by the commission."[33] A 1966 study by the Senate Subcommittee on Executive Reorganizing found that sixty percent of 15–19 year old African Americans in Watts believed that the police used excessive force. A similar study conducted by the University of California at Los Angeles (UCLA) in the same year, reported that seventy-four percent of blacks living in Watts thought that police officers engaged in various forms of brutality. Another study by the Urban League in Detroit found that eighty-two percent of the African American respondents believed that the police practiced some form of brutality.[34] Also in 1967, *A National Survey of Politics and Community Relations* was published and it noted that 43 out of 54 "formally recognized" black community leaders found police brutality to be the cause of poor community-police relations.[35]

Numerous instances of police brutality occurred during the 1960s and 1970s. In February of 1968, in Orangeburg, South Carolina, three unarmed African American students were killed by the police during a Civil Rights demonstration, and two more were killed on May 14, 1970 at Jackson State in Mississippi.[36] Even the conservative NAACP lashed out at urban police forces as infested with "racists and crooks." The NAACP maintained that only "lucky" African Americans could escape harassment by police in their lifetime.[37]

The notorious behavior of the Chicago Police caused the Rev. John Fry to debate the topic, "Is the Ghetto a Police State?"[38] A study by Ralph Knoohuizen, Richard P. Fahey and Deborah J. Palmer, published in 1972, found that African Americans in Chicago were six times as likely to be killed by a police officer as were whites.[39] In the early 1970s, the Western Center for Law and Poverty filed a class-action suit against the Los Angeles Police Department that charged the police with, "a systematic campaign of brutality and harassment against blacks."[40] Facts like these forcefully illustrate why the Panthers believed that a non-violent approach was impractical. As Newton stated, "What good, however, was nonviolence when the police were determined to rule by force?"[41] Given the historical context, then, it is very easy to see why the Black Panther Party believed so firmly in armed self-defense. The Panthers, in fact, asserted that the greatest threat to the well-being of African Americans was the police. Citing Fanon: "In the colonies it is the policeman and the soldier who are the official, instituted go-betweens, the spokesmen of the settler and his rule of oppression."[42] Panther Chief of Staff, David Hilliard, wrote, "The police mission isn't to serve and protect but to deny power to the people."[43]

The Denzil Dowell murder case is a vivid illustration of why the Panthers believed it was crucial to monitor the police. Dowell was killed by police officers in Richmond, California on April 1, 1967, after supposedly running from the police for stealing a car. The police reported that Dowell had jumped fences in his get-away attempt, but Dowell had sustained a hip injury years earlier in a car accident that made it impossible for him to do such things as jump a fence. Many members of the community sympathized with Panther co-founder Bobby Seale, when he stated that this was "just a cold-blooded killing of a black man." Huey Newton also noted in his dissertation years later, that no one, including the police, claimed that Dowell was armed.[44]

The Panthers were asked by the Dowell family to investigate the death of their son, partly because they believed that the police had murdered their son and partly because they believed that no one else would be willing to help them. The Party conducted an investigation and presented their findings to the Richmond Police Department, but no action was taken by the police or city officials.[45] The Panthers' lack of success in this matter did not mean their efforts were completely futile. The Black Panthers had demonstrated that they were more than willing to battle established institutions on behalf of African Americans, and that was invaluable.

The Panthers accepted the responsibility for monitoring the police because they knew it was illogical to report the wrongdoings of the police to the police. The Black Panthers stated that "the police have never been our protectors. Instead, they act as the military arm of our oppressors and continually brutalize us."[46] Numerous Party members believed that the police would not hesitate to kill an African American.[47] Many Black Panthers had first-hand knowledge of the ferocity of police forces across the country. The murder of seventeen-year-old Bobby Hutton by Oakland police on April 6, 1968, is yet another excellent example of police violence directed at the Panthers. The Party maintained that Hutton was shot seven times by the police, while his hands were in the air.[48]

One very graphic incident occurred in Chicago on December 4, 1969, when Chicago branch leader Fred Hampton, and Party member Mark Clark, were gunned down by the police in a hail of bullets, and four other Panthers were wounded. It was reported that Hampton had been killed while he lay in bed, drugged.[49] These murders were referred to as "nothing but a Northern lynching," by some African Americans in the community.[50]

The *University of Wisconsin-Milwaukee Crossroads* recognized that the Chicago branch were "victims of dangerous, contemptuous and even racist police actions."[51] An FBI ballistics expert determined that ninety shots had been fired, and that all but one came from the police. Hampton was shot four times, twice in the head. A study of Hampton's death, conducted by Roy Wilkins and former U.S. Attorney General, Ramsey Clark, concluded "that there is probable cause to believe that Fred Hampton was murdered."[52] The raid was conducted by fourteen police officers who were carrying a total of twenty-seven guns, including five shotguns and a submachine gun. It was just another instance of the police being "armed for overkill," as they were in so many of their Panther raids, and within the African American community as a whole.[53]

The Black Panthers tried to stem police brutality by patrolling the police in African American communities. The Party members who went on these patrols were armed so that they could adequately defend both themselves and members of their community if the need arose.[54] The Black Panthers stayed a reasonable distance from the police when they were making arrests. Their interest was in monitoring the arrest as it was being made, and advising the person being charged of their rights. The Party did not endorse violence against police officers, they were simply making it apparent that they were prepared to defend their neighborhoods and the rights of its citizens. This community service reinforced the popular misconception that the Panthers distrusted and hated all police officers. The Panthers only detested those police officers, black or white, who abused African Americans.[55]

The Black Panther Party realized, however, that countless other grave problems besides police brutality faced black communities. One major crisis the Party felt it had to address was the rampant hunger that existed among many poor, young African Americans. George McGovern illustrated the severity of the situation when he wrote:

> John Spargo shocked the nation with the publication of his book, 'The Bitter Cry of the Children' in 1906. Many questioned his statistics that in New York City alone, thousands of children went to school hungry everyday. . . . Unfortunately, John Spargo's accusations applied on a national basis, still ring true in January of 1972.[56]

In response to this situation, the Panthers initiated their Breakfast for Children Program in January of 1969.[57] The Panthers asked, "Why a breakfast for children program? The answers to this question need to be answered only for those who belong to the upper or so-called middle class."[58] The

Panthers knew they had to provide this service to their communities, because the government was not adequately addressing the problem. For instance, in 1967 only a meager $600,000 was spent nationally on breakfast programs by all levels of government. This figure increased to $2 million in 1968 and to $5.5 million in 1969. Fifty-thousand children nationwide benefited from free government breakfasts in 1967 and the number rose to 221,000 by 1969. These numbers may appear substantial, but many more children could have been fed. For instance, an estimated 3.5 to 6 million children qualified for free government breakfasts in 1972, but only 1.18 million were actually fed.[59] A number of reasons explain the inaction of the government ranging from bureaucratic red tape to lack of concern for the hungry. It was also reported that a number of breakfast program participants received nothing more than a carton of milk and a Twinkie-like substance known as "Astrofood." Astrofood supposedly was fortified with large dosages of vitamins and minerals, but it was routinely blasted by dietitians for lacking in nutritional value.[60]

The Panthers did not waste time in implementing their Breakfast for Children Program. As Fred Hampton said, "We (African Americans) need to do more acting than we do writing, and I think the Black Panther Party is doing that. We didn't talk about a breakfast for children program—we've got one."[61] The Program was designed to serve all children in elementary and middle schools. Usually located in neighborhood churches, such as the All Saints Catholic Church in Harlem, Saint Augustine Episcopal Church in Oakland, or the Forest Avenue Baptist Church in Des Moines, these stations offered free breakfasts to children before school started. Regardless of whether the parents of the children were Party members or if they were black, the Panthers fed them.[62]

The Breakfast Programs, like all Panther programs, were run by Black Panthers with financial assistance from local white and black businesspeople, as well as celebrities such as Marlon Brando, Jane Fonda and Bert Schneider. Breakfast for Children had varying degrees of success throughout the country. The Peekskill, New York and Los Angeles branches of the Panthers reported feeding 50 children a day, whereas a Chicago branch of the Black Panther Party provided 200 breakfasts daily and the Kansas City branch maintained that they fed 450 children a day. By the end of 1969, twenty-three branches, from New Haven, Connecticut to Oakland, California offered Breakfast Programs that served approximately 20,000 children a week. In 1972, Bobby Rush of the Chicago branch reported that 25,000 children were fed everyday nationwide by the Panthers' Breakfast Programs.[63]

The program was much more than a chance to get good publicity or new recruits for the Party. As Bobby Seale stated, "A true revolutionary will get up early in the morning and he'll go serve the free Breakfast for

Children."[64] Even FBI agents who monitored the Panthers, such as Curtis
R. Jimerson, were impressed by the Breakfast programs. Jimerson recognized that the Panthers were providing a valuable service to the African
American community. He believed that even if the Panthers were only feeding one child a day, it still would be a worthwhile project on their part.[65]
The Breakfast Program clearly illustrated that the Panthers were very concerned with the general well-being of black communities. The impressions
that the Panthers made with their Breakfast for Children Programs were
profound and can still be seen today. A number of Panther breakfast programs were eventually taken over by members of the community, as was
the case in Milwaukee.[66]

The Panthers also addressed the lack of adequate health-care facilities
for poor African Americans. For instance, the entire black community of
Watts, California did not have a single hospital until 1965.[67] Some physicians, such as Max Seham, stated that a "serious medical crisis" existed in
black communities. In 1973, author Pierre de Vise noted that "Americas
black ghettoes have but one-tenth of the physicians they need."[68] Clearly,
many African Americans needed better health care and the Panthers
attempted to fill that need. Ronald Satchel from the Chicago branch provided the Party's analysis:

> The medical profession is not responsive to the medical needs of the
> people and the medical profession within this capitalist society is com-
> posed generally of people working for their own benefit and advance-
> ment rather than the humane aspects of medical care.[69]

Newton and other Panther leaders dealt with this issue by founding their
own medical clinics. Free health clinics were established in 1969 in cities
such as Kansas City, Philadelphia, and Brooklyn. The clinics relied mainly
on monetary donations, as well as medical professionals from the surrounding community who volunteered their services. The Staten Island and Chicago branches of the Black Panther Party also had a free medical program
that centered on making housecalls. Most housecalls treated such ailments
as sickle-cell anemia, malnutrition, hearing and vision diseases and tooth
and gum diseases.[70]

A vital component of the Panther's medical clinics was testing for
sickle-cell anemia. The Black Panther Party believed they had to address the
problem of sickle-cell anemia because it disproportionately affected African
Americans. Historically, the sickle-cell trait was beneficial to people from
Africa and the Mediterranean, because this blood mutation helped to fight
off malaria. In the United States, however, malaria is obviously not a threat,

so over time, individuals with the sickle-cell became medically compromised. The *New York Times* reported in 1969, for example, that roughly 600,000 blacks in the U.S. were infected with this disease. The NAACP's publication, *The Crisis*, stated in 1971 that sickle-cell anemia affected 10 percent of African Americans. The *Bugle American*, an alternative Milwaukee newspaper, reported in 1972, that in the Milwaukee area alone, 12,000 blacks had sickle-cell anemia.[71] The Panthers had to provide this service to black Americans because no one else really seemed to be concerned. As former Panther, Akua Njeri, said, "Nobody (else) cared about things that affected us (African Americans), that were killing us, and that we were dying from."[72]

Another major problem facing African American communities at this time was the highly Eurocentric curricula of the public schools. Many Americans, black and white, could agree with Huey Newton that the public schools were sorely lacking in their efforts to meet the educational needs of African Americans. For example, in 1970, renowned sociologist, Kenneth Clark, and other scholars demanded a revision of teacher training curricula in order to make the teacher more aware of issues of diversity.[73] In 1973, the *Milwaukee Courier* wrote, "All the elements of the educational experience—staff, curriculum, materials, facilities—should be organized to contribute to the child's feeling that he is somebody valuable."[74] Out of these concerns, the Panthers decided to create their own schools. These schools would stress African American culture and history as well as the "standard" curriculum.[75] At these "Liberation Schools," as the Black Panthers called them, African American children were taught the accomplishments of their ancestors. Besides enhancing the self-esteem of the students, the schools taught both discipline and responsibility. The Liberation Schools also exposed the students to a more diverse curriculum than was being offered in mainstream schools.[76]

The first Liberation School opened in Berkeley, California on June 25, 1969. Some other branches, including Cleveland, San Francisco, San Jose, Seattle and Staten Island soon followed suit. The Oakland branch appeared to have the most success with these schools. Former head of the Panthers, Elaine Brown, reported that the Panthers had over 200 students enrolled, with a 400-person waiting list, at the Intercommunal Youth Institute in Oakland. Workers at the school also took students to get their dental and medical check-ups. Most other Liberation Schools reported that roughly twenty children attended everyday. In many cases, the school bought the children's school supplies for them as well as fed their daily meals.[77]

In addition, the Party also believed that it was scandalous for a college not to have some element of Black Studies, so the Panthers sought to have

African American Studies programs implemented throughout the country.[78] The Black Panthers believed that without Black Studies programs, colleges and universities were depriving African Americans from learning about their heritage and history. Therefore, the Panthers helped students on various campuses to mobilize and demand African American studies in their colleges. The Party was successful in having such programs implemented at San Francisco State, Merritt Junior College in Oakland, and Wilson Junior College in Chicago.[79]

Another illustration of the Panthers community service orientation was their Busing-to-Prisons Program. In 1974, Leo Carroll estimated that minorities made up nearly half of the prison population of the United States.[80] The Panthers believed that the highly discriminatory judicial system had incarcerated a disproportionate number of black Americans. Point number eight of the Black Panthers' Ten-Point Program (see Appendix A) called for the release of all African Americans held in prison, for the simple reason that they had not been tried by a jury of their peers. Realizing the unlikelihood of their demand being met, the Panthers had to deal with the situation as it stood. Panther chapters, such as those in Chicago and Boston, implemented a busing program for the relatives of prison inmates that provided poor families with the opportunity to visit their loved ones.[81]

The Panthers provided other valuable humanitarian services, such as the distribution of free groceries. The Black Panthers gave away 10,000 bags of food in the spring of 1972 in Oakland. Later that year they ran a nationwide Angela Davis Peoples' Free Food Program which distributed another 20,000 bags of groceries. In some instances the Panthers conducted small-scale food drives where they gave out baskets of food to those who came to the Party's office.[82] This distribution of free food is a clear representation of the Panthers' providing practical, essential services for black Americans throughout the United States.

Still another service the Party provided to black communities was the advice offered in the Party's newspaper, *The Black Panther*. First published in April, 1967, in Oakland, California, *The Black Panther* reached a circulation of nearly 100,000 a week in its effort to educate and inform, and to present a black perspective on a variety of issues. *The Black Panther* contained "legal first-aid" tips that were designed to familiarize the African American population with their constitutional rights. In some instances, the Panther employed kids, high-school dropouts and the local poor to sell the paper, which gave the salesperson as well as the Party a much needed source of income.[83]

The Black Panther Party also held a number of clothing drives to help those who could not afford clothes. Branches in Philadelphia, Seattle, New

Jersey and Oakland participated in these altruistic ventures. The New York chapter of the Panther Party stated that they had given away three tons of clothes to approximately 600 people.[84]

As an instrument of community organization, the Black Panthers attempted to negotiate gang truces to reduce the killings of African Americans.[85] Party members also tried to ensure the safety of blacks when they urged African Americans not to riot following the assassination of Martin Luther King, Jr. The Panthers realized that rioting accomplished nothing tangible, and that it only succeeded in having black people beaten and killed by the police and/or National Guard. Furthermore, the Panthers made a substantial effort to persuade Party members not to retaliate against Maulana Karenga's Us, even though Us was responsible for a number of deaths of Party members.[86] Black Panther leaders believed that retribution would only lead to further needless bloodshed among African Americans.

A housing protest by the Memphis branch caused the Memphis Housing Authority to immediately grant low-cost housing to ten impoverished black families who were living in condemned buildings. The Oakland branch provided employment for some people by manufacturing shoes at a shoe factory that the Panthers rented. Black Panthers offered voter registration assistance, posted bail for citizens from the black community, protested evictions of African American tenants, provided an escort and transportation service for senior citizens, offered a free plumbing program and they even offered free rat control. This multitude of services cost the Panthers roughly $100,000 a year by the Spring of 1973, which illustrates that these services were no small part of the Panthers' program.[87]

All told, the Black Panther Party offered a total of over thirty services and programs to African Americans. There were at least twenty-nine branches that offered breakfast programs, twelve that had health clinics and nine with Liberation Schools (see Appendix E). The sheer number of programs offered by the Party clearly demonstrates that the Black Panthers were the "oxen to be ridden by the people."[88]

This chapter has informed the reader of the Party's origins and goals, as well as the problems that the Panthers faced on the national level, thus providing a better understanding of the Party as a whole. In addition, by furnishing the reader with information about the Party on the national level, it becomes easier to see that the Milwaukee branch was not an aberration from the Party's overall mission of serving and protecting African American communities.

Chapter Three
The Black Panther Party in Milwaukee: A Case Study

Situated along the southwestern shores of Lake Michigan, Milwaukee was initially home to a variety of Native American groups, most notably the Potawatomi. In the mid-1650s, French traders and explorers began making inroads into the area now known as Wisconsin. Despite the encroachment of growing numbers of white settlers, Native Americans villages could still be found in the Milwaukee area by the early 1800s.[1] Upon completion of the Erie Canal in 1825, however, "streams of settlers" from New England poured into the Midwest to take advantage of the seemingly limitless availability of land as well as enhanced trading opportunities.[2] As more and more Europeans settled in the Milwaukee area, and throughout the Midwest, Native Americans were displaced to the west. Finally, in 1838, the Potawatami were forced to cede their land in the Milwaukee area to the United States Government through a series of treaties. Shortly thereafter, the Village of Milwaukee was established in 1839, primarily as a trading post.[3]

Milwaukee was a sparsely populated community from the outset, evidenced by its 1,712 inhabitants in 1840. Over the next 10 years, the Milwaukee population blossomed to 20,061 and the village became a city and also an industrial center, thanks to its close proximity to Lake Michigan and its shipping lanes. Milwaukee continued to witness tremendous growth in its population throughout the late 1800s, as numerous immigrants came in search of land for farming or low-skill industrial jobs. By 1910, Milwaukee's population had increased to 373,857.[4]

Prior to the 1920s, African Americans were a tiny population in the city of Milwaukee. As of 1890, there were only 158 African Americans in the city, and by 1910, less than 1,000 African Americans resided in Milwaukee.[5] As the Great Migration occurred, however, Milwaukee witnessed the influx of a substantial amount of African Americans who were in search of war-time work and greater socio-political freedom.[6] The Milwaukee black population jumped 125 percent between 1910 and 1920, but yet only numbered 2,346, or .5 percent of Milwaukee's general population.[7] As the Great Migration continued through the 1920s, Milwaukee's black population expanded by over 300 percent, and by 1930, 7,501 African Americans called Milwaukee home. Black migration to Milwaukee slowed down during the Great Depression, and by 1940, Milwaukee's black population was still only 8,700 out of 587,472 total residents.[8]

During, and after World War II, African Americans came to Milwaukee in large numbers once again, also in search of work created by the war effort, and a less overtly Jim Crow society.[9] Milwaukee's general population swelled to 637,392 by 1950, with more than 11,000 African Americans in the greater Milwaukee area.[10] The 1950s witnessed an immense expansion of the Milwaukee African American populace, as it grew to 62,458 by 1960, and comprised 8.4 percent of the city's population.[11] African Americans continued to come to Milwaukee throughout the 1960s, in search of the once plentiful industrial jobs that had largely been eliminated by automation, or replaced by low-pay service sector jobs. By 1970, Milwaukee boasted a population of 717,099 and a black population of 105,088.[12]

Numerous African Americans moved to Milwaukee in order to find opportunity and a less oppressive society, but many found a "very racist" society instead.[13] As Joe McClain, former president of the National Association for the Advancement of Colored Persons (NAACP) Commandos in Milwaukee, stated, "The only difference between racism here (the North) and in the South is that the southern racist is more outspoken, (whereas) the northern racist claims, 'I'm not racist.'"[14]

Illustrative of the racism present in Milwaukee was a study conducted by Peter Eisinger, an Urban Studies Professor at the University of Wisconsin-Madison, who discovered that the average household income for Milwaukee residents in 1960 was $7,000, but it was only $4,000 for African American families. To put this into perspective, the 1960 Conference on Economic Progress considered an annual income of less than $4000 as living in poverty. In fact, by 1970, 16 percent of Milwaukee African Americans still made under $3,000 annually, compared to only 7.5 percent of whites who made less than this paltry figure.[15] Black unemployment was also estimated at 2–3 times that of whites.[16] In addition to the disproportionately high rates of unemployment in Milwaukee was a highly segregated housing market. As of the 1960 census, the vast majority of African Americans in Milwaukee lived in an area of the city that was only 5.3 square miles.[17]

Further exacerbating the situation in Milwaukee were a white Mayor and Police Chief who were unsympathetic (at best) to the needs of the

Milwaukee African American population. Henry Maier served as Mayor of Milwaukee from 1960–1986, and during his long tenure, it was clear that he cared little for Milwaukee blacks, or any other minorities for that matter. Mark Braun, in his 1999 Ph.D. dissertation on Community Action Programs in Milwaukee in the 1960s, reaffirms this point when he states that, "It is likely that Maier . . . felt that low-income minorities could be ignored."[18] Local journalist, Frank Aukofer, claimed that "Henry Maier's communication with most of the established Negro Leadership in Milwaukee was almost nil."[19] Mayor Maier even denounced local civil rights activists, such as Father James Groppi, and blamed them for worsening the racial situation in Milwaukee.[20] Maier reflected the belief systems of his largely white working-class constituency that did not prioritize the concerns of its African American citizenry and Maier was determined to keep the support of his white voters. As Joe McClain states, "Maier was a politician who liked power. He would do anything to stay in power. Didn't matter if it was right or wrong."[21]

Unfortunately, Police Chief Harold Breier thought even less of the African American population than Maier. Throughout Breier's career as Chief it was apparent through his actions, and those of his officers, that he detested African Americans, as well as anyone who challenged the status quo. Breier joined the Milwaukee Police Department (MPD) in 1939 at the age of twenty-eight. He slowly worked his way up the ranks of the Department, before becoming Chief in 1964, a position he would hold until he retired in 1984.[22] Breier was thought of as an ideal person for the job, as he was viewed as a strict disciplinarian who would eliminate the corruption that plagued the Milwaukee Police Department in the early 1960s.[23] Breier was also characterized by many as an "active and aggressive officer" who would not hesitate to shoot at suspected criminals, evidenced by the fact that he fired his weapon at suspects on at least five different occasions.[24]

Coupled with Breier's aggressiveness was his latent bigotry which helped to foster a highly racist environment within the MPD. For instance, in 1965, a Milwaukee organization, the Citizens Anti-Police Brutality Committee, stated that "some law officers in this city constantly insult, harass and brutalize Milwaukee Negroes . . . every Negro is a second class citizen."[25] Reflecting Breier's bigotry, there were only 35 to 40 African Americans on the Milwaukee Police Force as of 1968, out of 2,000 total officers.[26]

The bigoted views of many Milwaukee police officers frequently manifested themselves in countless acts of police brutality against the African American population of Milwaukee. The Milwaukee Police Department's Tactical Squad was especially notorious for their brutality. Members of the Tactical Squad drove around with three or four officers to a car that was heavily armed with shotguns and rifles.[27] Sergeant Frank Miller of the Tactical Squad was regarded as one of the most ruthless members of the Milwaukee Police Department. Miller became so notorious that a local alternative newspaper, the *Kaleidoscope*, printed "wanted" signs with his picture on the front page.[28] Mark Braun maintains that "the tactical squad recruited 'outcast officers' from other departments who were considered overly aggressive." In addition, the Tactical Squad was usually the first unit at the scene of a civil disturbance, providing for a highly explosive situation.[29]

The Tactical Squad was not the only unit responsible for police brutality and misconduct in Milwaukee, as the countless allegations made by the African American community clearly illustrate. For example, fourteen-year-old Tyrone Dumas was allegedly beaten by Milwaukee Police in May of 1967. In July of the same year, the police reportedly kicked a pregnant mother and beat her sixteen-year-old son "like he was a dog."[30]

The brutality of the Milwaukee Police Department against African Americans was a main causal factor of the Milwaukee riot of 1967.[31] An editorial from the *Greater Milwaukee Star* helps to solidify this point:

> There are many reasons for urban unrest and tension. The unrest sets the pace for the civil disturbances that go on throughout the country, but in our fine city of Milwaukee, our so-called law enforcement institution is one of the largest sources in developing racial tensions in the inner city of Milwaukee with their Nazi-like tactics in the black community.[32]

The infamous riot took place on July 29, 1967 and lasted for three days. Over three hundred were injured and 186 were arrested. The Milwaukee riot was labeled the third worst civil disorder of the exceptionally turbulent year of 1967. Four people were killed, including an eighteen-year-old African American named Clifford McKissick.[33] McKissick's death further enraged the black community of Milwaukee, as McKissick had been shot in the throat by a Milwaukee police officer. The death was ruled "justifiable homicide," and the officer was not reprimanded. As Frank Aukofer notes, "To many Milwaukee Negroes, McKissick's death was simply another case of a white man killing a nigger and getting away with it."[34]

An even more disturbing facet of the riot was that local African Americans predicted a summer civil disturbance.[35] The city of Chicago received similar warnings from its black citizens, and the Chicago Police at least attempted to heed these concerns. Police officials in Chicago stated that "police officers were advised to use extreme skill and tact in handling situations that appear to be the first sign of tension situations."[36] Milwaukee Police Chief Breier, on the other hand, responded to community complaints with his typical bluster, "The officers (Milwaukee Police) will not back down at any time in the performance of their sworn duties."[37] The community was not asking for the police to deviate from their sworn duties, they just wanted a more humane police force.

In the wake of the riot, a 1967 study was conducted by Dr. Jonathan Slesinger of the University of Wisconsin-Milwaukee. Slesinger reported that 58 percent of the African Americans interviewed stated that the police were brutal in their dealings with the black community. In addition, 53 percent of black respondents in the study claimed that the police demonstrated lack of respect for Milwaukee African Americans.[38]

In 1968, the Survey Research Lab conducted a survey of 119 of the 186 people arrested in the Milwaukee riot. Out of the 119 surveyed, 95 were African American, 84 percent of whom testified that police brutality was a major cause for the riot. Only 24 percent of whites in the survey agreed with the aforementioned statement, however. The Survey Research Lab concluded "blacks in the general population, as well as arrestees, are more likely to say that police 'frequently' insult Negroes, unnecessarily frisk and search Negroes, beat people up, and the like."[39]

The 1968 Ad Hoc Committee on Police Administration in Milwaukee, comprised of local college professors, clergy and community representatives, also claimed that there were serious problems between the police and the Milwaukee black community. The Ad Hoc Committee stated that, "community-police relations with a large minority of our community are sorely strained, and tensions are mounting between citizens and police in the Central City."[40] In addition, in the same year, professors at local colleges and universities signed petitions demanding issues of police brutality to be recognized and dealt with accordingly. One such petition was signed by roughly 90 professors and instructors from the University of Wisconsin-Milwaukee (UWM), Alverno College, and Marquette University School of Medicine.[41]

Years later, the outspoken Michael McGee, a radical black military veteran and future Milwaukee alderman, noted that "the (Milwaukee) police were merely "the KKK in blue."[42] McGee is regarded by many local whites and blacks as a radical whose viewpoints usually fall outside the norm, but numerous others in the 1960s and 1970s echoed variations of McGee's acerbic assessment. For example, the UWM Student Chapter of the American Civil Liberties Union (ACLU) stated in 1970 that, "They (the police) are a tool of the repressive elements in society."[43] A 1970 study in

Milwaukee, conducted by Urban Observatories, revealed that 53 percent of African Americans surveyed were dissatisfied with the local government of Milwaukee, while only 11 percent of whites were. Another study, done by the University of Wisconsin Survey Research Lab in the same year, indicated that forty-four percent of blacks in Milwaukee were dissatisfied with law enforcement practices, but only nine percent of whites expressed the same sentiment. In fact, 38 percent of whites found law enforcement in Milwaukee to be highly satisfactory, yet only eight percent of African Americans felt the same way.[44]

In 1972, *The Bugle American*, reported that 85 percent of the African Americans they interviewed believed that "police brutality was a major cause of Breier's (Milwaukee Police Chief) riot."[45] And in 1973, local researchers Karl Fleming and John Ong, noted that Milwaukee blacks were "most dissatisfied with public safety services in their area."[46] By 1974, Bob Vernon, a columnist for the *UWM Post*, maintained that, "The police serve as an occupying force in these communities, to 'keep us in our places.'"[47]

The riot and the reaction of the police sparked outrage in many circles in Milwaukee, but the anger did not stop similar events from occurring in the future. In January of 1971, a pregnant Mary Mills claimed she was kicked by a police officer while under arrest, and in April, twelve-year-old Jeffrey Harris said he was beaten by the police. In October, thirteen-year-old Gaynor Morrison accused the Milwaukee Police Department of abuse, and in the winter of 1973, Clarence Euwing, a disabled military veteran, stated that he was beaten by the police.[48] In February of 1973, one African American was beaten so badly by the police, "that public officials were sickened by his appearance four days later."[49]

Harvey Martin reported that he was beaten by police on March 2, 1975 and David Butler was supposedly kicked by police while handcuffed inside a police van on October 23, 1976. Actions like these by the police caused headlines to read, "Black Men are being beaten to a pulp by Milwaukee's 'finest' everyday," and "Police Clubs Tenderize Black Heads."[50] As these examples also illustrate, the police did not restrict their brutality and misconduct to adult males.

Beyond this level of abuse, a number of black Milwaukeeans were reportedly killed by the police, only to have the deaths labeled "justified homicide."[51] The deaths of Daniel Bell in 1958, Clifford McKissick in 1967, Lee Wilson in 1968, Tommie Chesser in 1969, and Jacqueline Ford in 1972 were just a few among a larger number of African Americans who allegedly were gunned down by police.[52] These killings led additional headlines to read, "The Black community in Milwaukee is tired of trigger happy policeman in Milwaukee killing Black people at whim," and blacks were tired of

"Mississippi Justice." Police brutality and killings caused Wisconsin State legislator Isaac Coggs to note that Milwaukee was "worse than Dixie." While all of these incidents were occurring, police chief Breier maintained that police brutality did not exist.[53] Furthermore, Breier even denied that there was "need for improvement" in African American and police relations.[54]

Summing up Breier and the Milwaukee Police, some Milwaukee African Americans solemnly noted:

> It has taken a long painful time, but the conclusion is at last being forced upon the black population of the inner city that Chief of Police Harold A. Breier really does regard the black people of Milwaukee not only as an enemy, but as THE enemy.[55]

Clearly the city of Milwaukee needed to undergo substantial changes, and a variety of individuals and organizations were eager to take the lead.

Milwaukee, in fact, has a long rich history of African American protest. Two of the most senior Civil Rights activists in Milwaukee were Ardie Halyard (Clark) and Wilbur Halyard. The Halyards, originally from Atlanta, moved to Milwaukee in 1920 and helped organize the first branch of the NAACP there.[56] The Halyards remained activists throughout their lives, as they were still sitting on the Milwaukee NAACP Executive Board as late as 1961.[57]

The Milwaukee NAACP was very a vigilant organization, but it remained relatively small, with only 950 members as of 1947. As the Civil Rights Movement blossomed throughout the nation in the 1950s and 1960s, and as Milwaukee's black population swelled, however, Milwaukee's Civil Rights groups also grew. By 1966, the Milwaukee NAACP claimed a membership approaching 5,000. [58]

One dynamic individual that helped lead the Milwaukee NAACP through the 1960s was Lloyd Barbee, an African American lawyer and Wisconsin State Assemblyman for over 12 years. Barbee and the Milwaukee NAACP took their lead from the national NAACP in the 1960s, and therefore made the desegregation of schools one of their central objectives. The Milwaukee NAACP was not alone in their struggle to end school segregation, however, as they were soon joined in their efforts by the Milwaukee chapter of the Congress of Racial Equality (CORE).[59]

CORE emerged in Milwaukee in the Fall of 1963, and initially launched a series of sit-ins and marches protesting comments made by Fred Lins, a member of the Community Social Development Commission. The Commission was created by local officials in 1962, and one of its main objectives was to improve the conditions affecting the black populace in Milwaukee. Lins, however, was quoted as making statements such as, "An awful mess of them (African Americans) have an IQ of nothing," and "Negroes look so much alike that you can't identify the ones that committed the crime."[60] CORE's protest efforts against Lins were successful, as Lins resigned from the Commission in December of 1963.[61] After the Lins situation, CORE turned its attention towards the NAACP's school desegregation campaign.

In March of 1964, the Milwaukee chapter of CORE and the NAACP created an umbrella organization, the Milwaukee United School Integration Committee (MUSIC), to coordinate their school desegregation efforts, with Lloyd Barbee as the chair of MUSIC.[62] MUSIC staged massive picketing and leafleting campaigns in order to draw attention to the segregated school systems in Milwaukee. MUSIC also conducted a boycott of Milwaukee public schools, on May 18, 1964, in which 18,000 students stayed home from school in protest of the segregated system.[63] Barbee ultimately filed a lawsuit in Federal Court, on June 17, 1965, challenging the school segregation in Milwaukee. Eleven long years later, the Court ruled that Milwaukee Public Schools system was guilty of practicing de facto segregation.[64]

The Milwaukee NAACP not only had an energetic senior membership, they also had an incredibly active Youth Council. The Council was formed in Milwaukee in 1947 and it took part in many Civil Rights demonstrations throughout the city.[65] It was under the leadership of Father James Groppi in the mid-1960s, however, that the Youth Council became a major participant in the Milwaukee Civil Rights struggle.

Arguably the most well-known civil rights activist in Milwaukee during the 1960s and 1970s, and possibly ever, is the aforementioned Father James Groppi. Groppi was born in 1930 on Milwaukee's South Side to first generation Italian Americans. James Groppi's early childhood experiences prepared him for a life of social activism. He routinely defended himself against ethnic slurs and assault because he was an Italian American who lived in a predominantly Irish American neighborhood. Groppi and his family were even prevented from worshipping at the local Catholic church because of their ethnicity.[66]

Owing to his childhood experiences, as well as the influence of the Catholic Church, Groppi chose to attend St. Francis Catholic Seminary School in Milwaukee in 1952. He finished his schooling in 1959, and was assigned to St. Veronica's, an all-white Catholic Church on Milwaukee's South side. From the pulpit, Groppi denounced all forms of social wrongs, especially racial and ethnic discrimination. His sermons on racial tolerance irked many in his lily-white parish, and in 1963 Groppi was transferred to St. Boniface on Milwaukee's predominantly black north side.[67]

At St. Boniface, Groppi found an environment conducive to speaking out against racism. Groppi's rhetoric and his willingness to take on all issues of social justice, appealed to most churchgoers at St. Boniface, especially younger African Americans. A number of the young African American parishioners at St. Boniface were also members of the NAACP Youth Council, and Groppi quickly emerged as the advisor to the Council in July of 1965.[68]

Almost immediately, Groppi wanted the Council to tackle highly visible issues so that they could draw greater attention and support to their cause. Therefore, in 1966, the Council conducted widely publicized marches into Wauwatosa, a middle-class, overwhelmingly white suburb of Milwaukee, to protest the prestigious all-white Eagle's Club. Many bigoted whites in the Wauwatosa area did not appreciate the presence of Groppi and the Youth Council marchers. As a result, a number of Youth Council members were roughed up during their Wauwatosa march, and the Youth Council Freedom House was bombed by local members of the Ku Klux Klan on August 9, 1966.[69]

Amid the violence facing Groppi and the non-violent Youth Council, the Milwaukee NAACP Youth Commandos were formed in October of 1966. The Commandos, a select, interracial group, of roughly 150 members, played a pivotal role in protecting Groppi and the Youth Council, especially during the open-housing marches. The Commandos were a paramilitary organization, largely because many of the leaders of the Commandos were in the United States military at one time or another, and had adopted that method of organizing and mobilizing.[70] The Commandos did not carry weapons, but they still functioned as bodyguards for Groppi and the Council, and as organizers for the marches themselves.[71] As Joe McClain claims, the Commandos were trained never to instigate any fight or disturbance until "they (racists) put their hands on you."[72] If the Commandos or other marchers were attacked, the Commandos fought back. In fact, the Commandos learned to fight "pretty well in a crowd" as a result of routinely being surrounded by large groups of violent racists during the open-housing marches.[73]

On August 28, 1967, Groppi and the Youth Council and Commandos began the open-housing marches which continued for a number of months. The open-housing marches were in response to a highly segregated housing market in Milwaukee. In 1967, Velma Coggs, Treasurer of the Milwaukee Youth Council stated they "vowed to march for fair housing legislation in the City of Milwaukee until hell freezes over."[74] After over 200 nights of marching, in which the marchers were subjected to racial epithets and violence from bigoted citizens, and assaults and arrests from police officers, Mayor Maier, finally signed a open-housing ordinance on December 13, 1967.[75]

It was in this context of activism that the Black Panther Party also attempted to provide realistic solutions to the various ills that afflicted Milwaukee, particularly its African American residents. The Party emerged in Milwaukee in 1969, coinciding with the "peak period" of the Black Panther Party nationally.[76] The Panthers believed that marches, like those of Groppi and the Youth Council, would not bring sufficient and timely changes to the many grave problems gripping the African American community of Milwaukee.[77] In addition, a number of Milwaukee Black Panthers, such as Booker Collins, Donald Young and Ronald Starks, also were Vietnam veterans who possessed a sense of militancy that could not be placated by marching and sit-ins.[78] The Panthers believed in direct-action programs that provided immediate and tangible results for the people. The Black Panther Party of Milwaukee also wanted to be more than bodyguards, which was what the Commandos appeared to be.

According to FBI records, the Panthers attempted to organize in Milwaukee as early as December 3, 1968, but were not firmly established until January of 1969, when they rented an office at 829 West Atkinson Avenue. By June of 1969, the Panthers were forced out of their West Atkinson address, as the landlord of the property on West Atkinson had finally realized that his tenants were the "radical" Black Panthers.[79] Subsequently, the Milwaukee branch moved their base of operations to 2121 North 1st Street. The Panther office was open seven days a week, from noon until 8 p.m., attempting to serve the black people of Milwaukee.[80]

The Milwaukee Panthers emphasized that, "The primary objective of the Black Panther Party was to bring the entire black community together to work on common problems."[81] In addition, the Milwaukee branch also stressed the importance of engaging in self-defense. For instance, Panther member John Trenton stated that the Party "will take no acts of aggression but we're going to defend ourselves."[82]

The Panthers also placed emphasis on recruiting women into the Panther Party. The Milwaukee branch, however, appeared to have some initial difficulty in persuading women to join the Party. Reflective of the desire to get more women involved in the Party, in June of 1969, branch member Lovetta X made a spirited plea that urged black women to get involved in the Party. Lovetta X did caution potential female recruits though, when she stated, "Sisters, (you) got to be ready. If you're scared, then you better stay where you are. We don't need you."[83]

The Black Panther Party in Milwaukee, similar to the Party at the national level, believed in working coalitions with all ethnic groups "as long as it's for humanity."[84] As branch Captain, Dakin Gentry stated, "We're not advocating racism in any form."[85] Gentry also said, "We will work with anyone that shows a sincere interest in trying to help the black man overcome his problems . . . be they black or white."[86]

Unlike the Black Panther Party at the national level, however, the Milwaukee Panthers also had working coalitions with black cultural nationalist organizations. Milwaukee's decision to work with cultural nationalist organizations is rather surprising, given that the national leadership of the Black Panther Party detested cultural nationalists. The Milwaukee branch, however, worked with cultural nationalist groups such as The Black Arts Theater, which sought to advance black pride and cultural awareness through the performance arts. The Party also worked with the Go-For-Soul Committee, which stressed the need for a more Afrocentric curricula in Milwaukee schools. In addition, the Party joined forces with Commandos Project I, a program that emphasized black unity.[87]

When the Black Panthers came into existence in Milwaukee, Joe McClain of the Commandos told them that "the police were going to come down hard on them (the Panthers)," because of the Panther's strong militancy.[88] Unfortunately, McClain was very astute in his assessment of the Milwaukee Police force. Almost immediately after opening in the Milwaukee community, the Panthers were besieged by the FBI and an aggressive local police force that was determined to eliminate the Black Panther Party as a viable organization in Milwaukee.

Given the early history of the Panthers on the national level, the Milwaukee branch also knew that the authorities would soon come for them. Therefore, the Panthers fortified the doors of their headquarters with sheet metal, and placed wire mesh over all the windows. In addition, the Party reserved most of their important conversations for in the car, where the chance of wiretaps was minimal.[89] All of these defensive measures would little avail the Milwaukee Party, however.

The Black Panther Party in Milwaukee were "outwardly confronting the power structure in the name of oppressed Black people," and the 1969 Milwaukee Panthers paid a heavy price for doing so.[90] For example, in March of 1969, Walter Chesser, Deputy Minister of Defense of the Milwaukee Panthers and brother of Tommie Lee Chesser, alleged that he was beaten by police for no apparent reason other than being a Panther.[91] In early June of 1969 Nate Bellamy, Lieutenant of Information of the Milwaukee branch, had his car rammed by the police, causing him to be hospitalized and arrested for allegedly carrying a concealed weapon. Bellamy was handcuffed to his hospital bed, while six Milwaukee police officers guarded his room making sure that no one could visit him.[92] Later in June, four Milwaukee Panthers were arrested for carrying loaded handguns, and held in jail with bail set at $350 apiece. Three of the four Panthers were then sentenced to 90 days in jail, and the fourth had the charges dismissed because he was a juvenile.[93]

The worst spell of persecution occurred in September of 1969, where within a span of forty-eight hours, six Panthers were incarcerated on two separate incidents. The first incident, three Party members were stopped for a traffic violation. Eyewitnesses to this episode said that three Panthers were viciously beaten during the arrest. One Panther was supposedly beaten by an officer while two other police officers held his arms. When Panther Field Lieutenant Felix Welch finally was able to visit the three Panthers he "almost got sick to his stomach," because of their grotesque physical appearance as a result of the beating.[94]

The other arrest was of the locally infamous Milwaukee Three. Three Panthers, Booker Collins, Jesse White and Earl Levrettes, supposedly tried to murder Robert Schroder, a Milwaukee police officer, in September of 1969. According to Schroder, the three Panthers drove up behind him while he was walking his "beat" on Fond Du Lac in the early morning hours. One of the Panthers supposedly pointed a shotgun at Schroder and fired. Miraculously, Schroder had the presence of mind to drop to the ground just in time to avoid the shotgun blast, but he also claimed that he saw the gun discharge. Not only did Schroder exhibit cat-like reflexes, but then he had the presence of mind to write down the license plate number of the car as it sped away.[95] Those in the community who knew the Milwaukee Three firmly believed that the Three had more sense than to roam around the city looking for random cops to kill.[96] The Three claimed that they did not even have a shotgun in the car when they were later pulled over by the police for the attempted shooting of Schroder. According to the Three, however, one officer, with a shotgun in hand, went over to the van, and then came out of the van with the same shotgun, and said, "Here, I found a shotgun."[97]

The three contended that after they were arrested they were all brutally beaten six separate times within twenty-four hours, while wearing handcuffs. A reporter from the *Milwaukee Courier* who interviewed the Milwaukee Three shortly after their arrest, said that there was no doubt the Three were beaten, evidenced by all the bruises and swelling on their faces.[98] In addition to the physical beating, the three were found guilty by an all-white jury, and Collins and White were given thirty-year sentences, while Levrettes was given ten.[99]

Further crippling the party were the arrests of Panther members George Owens and Allen Crawford in October of 1969, for supposedly carrying concealed weapons. The Panthers pleaded not guilty, but were found guilty by Judge Ryan Duffy, who sentenced them to ninety days in jail.[100]

In addition to the oppressive local police force, the Milwaukee branch also had to contend with the efforts of the FBI, that demanded that "Constant and aggressive actions be taken to fully penetrate the Black Panther organization in Milwaukee."[101] The FBI in Milwaukee also sought a "vigorous investigation" in regard to the Panther's Breakfast for Children Program in order to "develop areas for effective employment of counterintelligence measures."[102]

Largely as a result of the external pressures exhibited on the Milwaukee Panthers, the Milwaukee branch was dissolved by the Black Panther Party's Central Committee in November of 1969. Before being disbanded, however, the Milwaukee Panthers of 1969 reached a highly respectable 75–100 active members.[103]

Despite all the difficulties that faced the Milwaukee Panthers in 1969, the Black Panther Party was not completely finished in Milwaukee. In April of 1972, Ronald Starks, Lieutenant of Education of the original Milwaukee Panthers, and Michael McGee, formed the People's Committee to Free Jan Starks. Jan, Ron's brother, was a soldier in the military, who was imprisoned in Taiwan for allegedly possessing opium.[104] There was the firm belief in many circles that Starks was framed because of his race and low military rank. For instance, Wisconsin Congressman, Henry Reuss, regarded the case as nothing more than a "frameup."[105]

After Jan Starks was freed, thanks to efforts by People's Committee, the larger African American community, and Reuss, Ronald Starks and McGee sought to create a more permanent organization that would revolve around serving the African American community of Milwaukee. On April 22, 1972, the two helped to form the People's Committee for Survival, which was predicated on community service.[106] Although the Committee had no official affiliation with the Black Panther Party, the People's Committee did not hide their devotion to the ideals of the Party. As Kenneth Williamson, the Committee's Minister of Information, stated, "We (the People's Committee) accept the ideology and follow the leadership of the Black Panther Party."[107]

After the Committee became a stable organization, it applied for a Black Panther Party charter, which it received one-and-a-half years after applying. In August of 1973, a Panther branch was re-established in Milwaukee under the leadership of Starks and McGee. The major reason it took so long to receive the charter, was because the Panther Central

Committee was hesitant to grant another charter in Milwaukee, given its past history. Therefore, the Central Committee wanted to wait and see if the People's Committee was a stable organization deserving of a charter.[108]

The "second wave" of the Black Panthers in Milwaukee peaked at fifty members, yet reported a membership as low as ten at one point. Much like the Black Panther Party across the nation, the Milwaukee branch also had a significant representation of women within the branch. In fact, according to Panther leader, Michael McGee, the Milwaukee branch probably had a few more women members than male members. [109] The membership was comprised of individuals from fairly diverse backgrounds, ranging from students, to city workers, to ex-prostitutes.[110] As with the "first wave" of the Black Panthers in Milwaukee, the Milwaukee branch also formed numerous coalitions with other revolutionary organizations. For instance, the Party had very beneficial alliances with predominantly white groups such as SDS and the Patriots.[111]

Just like the earlier Milwaukee branch, the 1973 Black Panthers also had their share of difficulties with the law enforcement agencies. For instance, the MPD assigned the "Red Squad" to investigate the Panthers. The Red Squad was essentially Breier's local equivalent of J. Edgar Hoover's COINTELPRO. The Squad was a small, select unit that followed, harassed, and kept hidden files on local radicals, including the Panthers.[112]

In addition to the constant surveillance by the Milwaukee Police, and especially the Red Squad, the FBI attempted to sabotage the Milwaukee branch. For instance, much like at the national level, the FBI spread negative rumors among possible allies of the Black Panther Party, such as various black churches as well as the Nation of Islam. Furthermore, the FBI frequently broke into the Panther's headquarters in an effort to uncover incriminating information about the Party.[113]

The FBI also placed informants in the Milwaukee branch. As Michael McGee claimed, FBI infiltration was so frequent that "you almost had to expect [sic] everyone who came in."[114] In addition, the FBI purposely uncovered one of the informants, "Barry," in an effort to get the Panthers to kill Barry, so that the Party could be charged with murder. Unfortunately for the FBI, the Panthers did not kill Barry, but they did expel him.[115]

The Black Panthers in Milwaukee began to whither away by 1976, largely due to police repression. And in 1977, Huey Newton shut down all branches outside of California in an attempt to limit infiltration by law enforcement agencies. As a result, many members of the Milwaukee Panthers merged into a local umbrella organization, the United Black Community Council (UBCC). The UBCC was a fairly diverse Black Power organization, as it incorporated ex-Panthers as well members of the Republic of New

Africa and the National of Islam. The UBCC existed for roughly ten years until it collapsed, largely due to an ideological struggle among the members, as many tried to make the UBCC adhere to only one ideology.[116]

Even though the history of the Milwaukee Black Panther Party is a very torrid one because of police harassment, as well as internal dissension, the Party did clearly illustrate that their main concern was to serve the people.[117] The Party provided a wide variety of services to the lower-income African American population of Milwaukee, and those programs will be the subject of the next two chapters.

Chapter Four
Providing for All

The Black Panther Party is routinely portrayed as an ultra-militant group that was fixated on armed warfare with the police and the government. Yet, an examination of the Black Panther Party in Milwaukee yields a much different perspective of this controversial organization. The Black Panther Party in Milwaukee was a community-oriented organization dedicated to providing a variety of formal and informal programs and services to lower-income African American residents. For instance, the Party placed great emphasis on community control of the police as part of their larger efforts to improve police-African American relations. The Panthers also initiated a very successful Busing to Prisons Program and they operated their own health center, known as the People's Free Health Clinic. In addition, the Milwaukee branch of the Black Panther Party provided an array of miscellaneous services and programs to the community illustrating that serving the black community of Milwaukee was of primary concern.

Following the national Black Panther Party line (see point number two in Appendix A), the Milwaukee Black Panthers attempted to address the problems of police brutality in a number of different ways, without resorting to violent means. Milwaukee Panther Walter Chesser noted that the Panthers "have the gun as merely a defensive tool." Michael Walker, an assistant to Mayor Henry Maier, also wrote, "The Party has no wish to create any civil disorder in the Community, but such problems as police brutality, or any problems of this nature, the Party will intervene and try the rectify the problem with the best means possible."[1]

In October of 1969, reflecting the Party's desire to stem police brutality without using violence, the Black Panther Party of Milwaukee began their push for the decentralization of the Milwaukee Police Department with the ultimate aim of greater community control. The Panthers noted that "the trend in law enforcement by the Milwaukee Police Department has been toward arbitrary and unequal enforcement of the law to the detriment of the poor, the propertyless, minority groups, and especially Black persons."[2] The Party and many Milwaukee citizens believed that police "king" Breier exercised too much power and this power needed to be given back to the people.[3] The Milwaukee Panthers, according to Nate Bellamy, sought to remove "all these fascist, racist storm troopers (Milwaukee Police) and, in turn, replace them with some respectable new police officers."[4] The Party knew, however, that there were dedicated police officers in the Milwaukee Police Department. As Nate Bellamy noted, the Panthers, "realize that there are some people on the police force, unfortunately, who are actually dedicated to the people's needs," but these officers could not adequately serve the people for fear of losing their jobs under Breier's racist administration.[5]

The Panther's proposal called for the creation of separate police departments for the white, black and brown communities. The Party firmly believed that under their new system, the police would be more representative of the areas which they lived in, and therefore more in-tune to the needs of the community under the Party's plan.[6] Each department would be administered by a commissioner who was selected by a fifteen-member "neighborhood police control council."[7] Ronald Starks noted that these fifteen would select regional police commissioners, as opposed to the single administrator model.[8] Members of the neighborhood police control councils would be elected by their own communities. In addition, police officers, commissioners and council members would be subject to recall if they did not perform their duties sufficiently for the community.[9] As Dakin Gentry claimed, "The people should control everything," not racist and dictatorial police chiefs such as Harold Breier.[10]

Not only did the Panthers call for greater community involvement in the selection and oversight of the police, the Panthers also wanted police officers patrolling the area in which they lived. The Party maintained that community policing would create better community-police relations as well as lessen the case-load of overburdened courts. The Panthers claimed that many cases resulted from police officers abusing their authority and arresting people on petty or trumped-up charges. The Black Panthers logically believed that these officers would not be as likely to behave in such a fashion in their own neighborhoods. Furthermore, according to the Party's plan, the Milwaukee police force would inevitably become more ethnically diverse if police officers were chosen from all sections of the highly segregated community of Milwaukee.[11]

When the Black Panther Party was disbanded in Milwaukee in November of 1969, the remaining Panther members were told by the Party's national leadership to organize under the newly formed National Committee to Combat Fascism (NCCF). The national leadership of the Black Panther Party realized that there needed to be one organization that coordinated the efforts of myriad different organizations of the sixties, while simultaneously recognizing the autonomy of each organization. Therefore, the Party sponsored a conference in July 1969, at which time the NCCF was formed. The NCCF was an umbrella organization that incorporated such groups as the Students for a Democratic Society, the Brown Berets and Young Lords, as well as various women's and gay liberation organizations.[12] Despite having varying ideologies and concerns, one constant factor that bound all groups together was that they all faced varying levels of police persecution, therefore the NCCF emphasized community control of the police in order to stem police repression.

Roughly forty branches of the NCCF sprouted up throughout the United States during 1969–1970, including one in Wisconsin. Formed in 1970, the Wisconsin Committee to Combat Fascism (WCCF) carried on the Panther's efforts for the decentralization of the police. For example, in 1970, the WCCF circulated petitions to the Milwaukee Common Council, urging the Council to take power away from Chief Breier and give it to local communities.[13] The WCCF also sent out a six-page letter in 1970 to various community organizations, stating their platform for community control of the police. Among the demands of the WCCF, was the call for:

> The establishment of neighborhood (police) districts throughout the city. The districts shall be divided to reflect the economic, cultural, ethnic, and racial makeup of the various neighborhoods of the city. Each district shall have neighborhood police control councils which will select the police commissioner from the district and will have the power to review police policy as it effects the neighborhood district, including the power to discipline police officers for breach of department policy.[14]

According to the WCCF, their proposal would remove "the one-man dictatorship of Chief Breier" and give the power where it belongs, in the hands of the people.[15]

The WCCF's efforts were largely futile, as the WCCF struggled to gain notoriety during an era of immense organizational activity. Therefore, the Party once again took the lead in the decentralization campaign after they were officially re-established in Milwaukee in August of 1973. The Black Panther Party may have led the struggle for community control of the police, but they also sought to incorporate as many different people and groups into their struggle as possible. For instance, the Panthers worked in concert with Westside and Eastside whites, as well as Southside Latinos.[16]

In May of 1974, the Panthers publicly announced a plan (see Appendix D), that would allow citizens to elect a multiracial governing council of fifteen people, known as the Citywide Police Commission. The elections would be "low budget" elections, so that rich candidates could not buy an election.[17] The city government would allot every candidate a small amount of funds for his or her campaign. Those elected would have to be eighteen, not hold any other public office, and not be on the Milwaukee Police force at that particular time. Ronald Starks also stated that "these district citizen boards will have control over hiring and firing, promotions, citizen complaints, grievances and internal investigations of the police department."[18] The records and meetings of the Citywide Police Commission would be easily accessible to the public and citizens could petition for special meetings to take place.[19] Starks went on to state, "Community control of the police will make the policeman a community protector instead of an oppressive force used against the people."[20]

The Party set a goal of 30,000 signatures for a 1976 referendum that would request State Legislators to change the laws governing police affairs.[21] The Panthers were not successful in 1976, but their work somewhat paid off with the passage of Assembly Bill 42 in July of 1977. Assembly Bill 42, which limited the terms of police and fire chiefs to 10 years, passed the State Assembly and Senate in April of 1977, and acting Governor Martin Schreiber signed the Bill into law in July of that year.[22] The Black Panther Party was not directly credited with the passage of Bill 42, but it is arguable that without the community organizing and the attention that the Panthers brought to the issue, Bill 42 would never have passed.

Unfortunately, illustrating Chief Breier's power, Milwaukee police and fire chiefs were omitted from Bill 42's restrictions.[23] Despite the failure of Panthers to reduce Breier's power, the Party was successful in helping to make other Wisconsin communities more democratic in terms of their police and fire departments. Furthermore, the Party should not be judged in terms of their success, but in terms of their commitment to helping working-class African American communities. As the prolonged battle for the decentralization of the Milwaukee Police Department illustrated, the Party was devoted to helping the lower-income populace of Milwaukee.

The Milwaukee Common Council finally stripped Breier of much of his power in 1984, however, including lifetime tenure, after the heavily publicized killing of Ernest Lacy in 1981. Milwaukee police beat the 22-year old Lacy, an African American, in the back of a police van. Public outcry was so severe that the Common Council felt compelled to act, and thus divvied up Breier's power among the Common Council, the Mayor, and Fire and Police Commissions. In typical Breier style, he retired rather than serve with diminished authority. Lacy's family was given a paltry $600,000 by the city of Milwaukee for this wrongful death.[24]

Further illustrating their dedication to providing for the lower-income black community of Milwaukee, the Milwaukee branch created a very successful Free Busing to Prison Program. The Busing Program, initially created on June 9, 1972, by the People's Committee for Survival, became a Panther program when the Party formally returned to Milwaukee.[25] The Panthers, and the larger African American community, recognized a real and immediate need for this service. Ronald Starks rhetorically asked, "Just because a Brother or Sister commits a crime, is it correct for them to be cut off from their loved ones, friends and community with no communication?"[26] Buses carried between 150 to 200 people every Sunday from the Party's office at 3287 North Green Bay Avenue and later from 2470 North 3rd Street, to the relatively distant Wisconsin prisons in Waupun, Green Bay, and Fox Lake.[27]

The Panthers had a number of difficulties maintaining the busing service. First, P & R Bus Service ceased supporting the efforts of the People's Committee when the Committee changed the name of the service from "The People's Committee for Survival Free Busing to Prisons Program" to "The Milwaukee 3 Free Busing to Prisons Program," in honor of the Milwaukee Three.[28] Apparently P & R did not want to be associated with the Milwaukee Three's controversial court case or the Black Panther Party for fear of economic reprisals.

In addition, the high cost of the Busing Program also caused many problems. Ronald Starks estimated that it cost the Panthers at least $600 a month to run three buses to prisons that were roughly 60 to 100 miles away. According to Michael McGee, the Busing Program was the most expensive program that the Panthers offered, costing them roughly $450 per trip to Green Bay, and $180 per trip to the other Wisconsin prisons. Contributions from various individuals and bookstores, such as Rhubarb's, a locally owned bookstore, helped finance the Busing to Prisons Program, but the Panthers were constantly in short supply of funds for the Busing Program. The exorbitant cost of the program forced the Panthers eventually to downsize it from a weekly service, to a bi-weekly service by 1974.[29]

The Panthers initially did receive roughly $2,000 in funding for the Program from Milwaukee Hunger Hike, a local non-profit organization, but Hunger Hike stopped funding the program as soon as they realized that the People's Committee was, in fact, the Black Panther Party.[30] A letter dated June 10, 1974 from Hunger Hike to the Milwaukee Panthers, states that Hunger Hike could not give additional funds to the Party because,

"The Milwaukee Hunger Hike, a charitable, non-profit organization, cannot by law fund a political party of any type."[31] Even though the People's Committee and the Black Panther Party differed only in name, that was reason enough for Hunger Hike to cease funding the Program.

The People's Committee also tried to procure a bus of their own for this venture. The Committee sent out letters to various individuals and organizations requesting donation of funds to buy a 1958 Greyhound bus for $13,500, instead of renting a bus for $4,940 a year. The People's Committee, however, was not successful in procuring the necessary funds.[32]

The Busing to Prisons Program was an invaluable service to a number of Milwaukee African American families. As Michael McGee noted, the Party was enabling prison inmates to stay tied-in to the community and their families, and not become disengaged from it.[33] Illustrating the success of the Busing Program, one prison inmate remarked that the sheer numbers of participants in the program illustrated that "the high price of travel is the reason that many people do not visit their relatives and friends."[34] The Busing to Prisons Program, like the Party's sustained efforts for the decentralization of the MPD, illustrates the Panthers deep concern with providing social services to a large segment of the Milwaukee African American populace.

Another pressing problem facing the low-income black community of Milwaukee in the 1960s and 1970s was the lack of adequate health care. The North side of Milwaukee, home to many of the city's African Americans, lost its emergency hospital facilities in May of 1970. The loss of emergency facilities forced local newspaper headlines to read, "Community needs emergency hospital facilities immediately!" and "emergency hospital facility vitally needed."[35] Various stop-gap solutions were implemented, but the North side had to wait until August of 1972 before substantial emergency facilities were at their disposal. Even after the facilities were built, many people did not have the financial resources to use the services at an estimated $13.75 per visit. In addition to not being able to afford the health services, many still found the health care on the North Side atrocious.[36] For example, in 1975, columnist Cal Patterson from the *Milwaukee Courier*, remarked that helpful doctors in the African American community were viewed as a "luxury."[37]

It was in this context that ex-Panthers attempted to meet the medical needs of the lower-income populace of Milwaukee. In late 1969, the Black Panthers claimed that they were trying to set up a medical clinic in the black community. The Black Panthers, however, were dissolved less than two months after making this statement.[38] Despite lacking ties to the official organization, ex-Panthers established the People's Free Health Center in late 1970, at 1348 N. 27th Street. The Free Health Center proved to be a much needed social service, as it reported serving roughly 2,000 people by 1972. The demand of the People's Health Center also stretched across racial and ethnic lines, as the People's Center reported that 60 percent of its clientele were white, 30 percent were African American, and the remaining 10 percent were Chicanos. Unfortunately, the building that housed the Health Center was heavily damaged by a fire in November of 1972, thus putting a temporary end to the Free Health Center.[39]

Ex-Panthers and members of the People's Committee for Survival realized that the community still needed affordable health care, and therefore started up the new People's Free Health Center in early 1973, at 2636 North 3rd Street.[40] Coordinator of the Health Center, Geneva McGee, stated that "all medical care at the Clinic will be provided to the patient free. We believe that good health care is the right of all people and not a privilege of the wealthy."[41] The Health Center was ran by two paid staffers, McGee, and Charlotte Nash, as well as roughly twenty volunteers. Most of the volunteers were white doctors and dentists, who donated their time free of charge. For instance, a medical resident at Milwaukee Children's Hospital allotted his Monday evenings, free of charge, for children referred to him by the Center.[42]

The People's Free Health Center also sponsored health orientation programs, which educated the community on a variety of health issues such as sickle cell anemia, drug abuse, children's health and birth control. Furthermore, the Center served as a place for general social issues to be discussed as well, such as relationships between black men and women, and the need for unity among black youth.[43] The Panthers did not expect the Center to be a fully functional hospital, they merely hoped that the clinic would serve as "entry point into the medical system."[44] In other words, the Panthers provided preventative health care. As the *Milwaukee Courier* reported, "Many of the people reached by the Center know little about doctors and hospitals and have used them only in emergencies."[45]

By 1976, the Free Health Center gave high blood pressure screenings every weekday, except Tuesdays, from 1–6 p.m. As with testing for sickle-cell anemia, the Panthers realized that high blood pressure was a serious concern among African Americans. According to the Center, one out of ten blacks suffered from high blood pressure.[46]

Much like the Busing to Prisons Program, the People's Health Center was continually in desperate need of funds. As of 1975, the only regular financial assistance for the Health Center, came from Milwaukee's Social Development Commission, and even that was quite minimal. Due to severe financial constraints, clinic services were suspended for several months in

1975 mainly because the Center was unable to afford "skyrocketing" malpractice insurance.[47]

In 1975, the People's Health Center, in conjunction with representatives from nearby St. Mary's Hospital, applied for funds from the University of Wisconsin-Madison's Physician Residency Program, in order to establish a more permanent People's Health Center with greater resources. The application for funding was denied because the Health Center only had a nurse practitioner as the primary administrator.[48] Despite this temporary setback, "while the St. Mary's and People's Center proposal was never accepted, adopted, and put in place, elements of it continued to be discussed."[49]

The proposal by the People's Health Center served as the impetus for the creation of the Harambee Health Task Force, with Geneva McGee as a representative. The Harambee Task Force drafted a proposal that helped create the Isaac Coggs Community Health Center, which opened to the public in 1980. The Coggs Center gave complete check-ups, as well as blood, urine, hearing, blood pressure, pregnancy and glaucoma screenings, at no charge.[50] It is important to note that the roots of the Coggs Center "extend back before the Harambee Health Committee coalesced, back to the turbulent 1960s when many people, particularly those who were black and of middle to low income, realized the necessity of controlling their own lives."[51] The origins of the Coggs Center, in fact, extend back to the creativity and vision of the Black Panther Party.

In addition to the formal programs of the Panthers, the Party also provided a wide array of informal community services that further demonstrated their commitment to serving the lower-income African American population in Milwaukee. For example, the Panthers did mundane tasks, such as filling in potholes at the corner of First and Wright in March of 1969, because the Party found the potholes dangerous for children on bikes.[52] The Party also volunteered their headquarters on occasion as temporary housing for black tenants who were unfairly evicted. In addition, the Panthers published a local *Black Panther* newsletter by June of 1969 that served to inform and educate the African American community of Milwaukee.[53] The initial run of the newsletter was a "well-written" six-pages, and ultimately had a circulation of 3,000 copies.[54]

This militant Black Power group also engaged in traditional civil rights-style demonstrations, such as their protest of the segregationist policies of the Oasis Theater in June of 1969. The Oasis was previously picketed by the Organization of Organizations (Triple O), a local community organization, for overselling their films and for frequent showings of adult films.[55] More importantly, The Oasis also made young African Americans sit in the aisles to make room for white customers when necessary. When confronted by the Party about their Jim Crow practices, the Oasis management responded that they engaged in such actions because the Oasis viewed young blacks as troublemakers. The Party retaliated by staging peaceful demonstrations outside the theater. During the course of the Panther's protest, the Milwaukee Police Department arrived and promptly arrested three Panthers, Lynn Epps, Dakin Gentry, and Jesse White, for supposedly blocking the entrance to the theater. Despite the setback, the Party did achieve a satisfactory agreement with the theater owner that stated that the Panthers would speak with the kids about behaving, and, in turn, the owner would allow the children to sit in seats.[56]

The Panthers also picketed I & L Foodstores in late June of 1969. A number of people from the community complained that the store set prices too high, because the store knew that people in the community had no other nearby option for grocery shopping. I & L, located at 2636 North 3rd Street, catered to a predominantly poor, black community that lacked the resources to travel elsewhere to shop.[57] While protesting outside of I & L, four Black Panthers were arrested and charged with disorderly conduct and violating the city's panhandling laws. The Panther's protest did not cause I & L to lower their prices, but the protest did persuade I & L to contribute to the Party's Breakfast Program.[58]

Ex-Panthers carried on their community improvement efforts in the People's Committee for Survival, evidenced by the giveaway of 1,000 bags of food at Malcolm X Park in late 1972. The food distribution "was a conscious emulation of the (national) Black Panther Party's giveaway of 10,000 bags of food in Oakland that same year."[59] After the People's Committee became the Black Panthers, the food distribution efforts continued, but on a much lesser scale, as the Party gave out a bag of groceries to a small group of needy families on a weekly basis.[60]

By September of 1973, the Milwaukee Black Panthers ran a small child care facility at their headquarters, as well as an egg co-op, where they sold eggs at wholesale out of their office. The Panthers also unsuccessfully attempted to set up a community blood bank to sell pints of blood to the community at a fraction of what it was sold for at hospitals.[61] Apparently, a pint of blood cost $35 at area hospitals. Therefore, the Panthers suggested that people could donate blood at the Party's headquarters, and then individuals could buy the blood for $15 per pint.[62]

Furthermore, the Panthers wanted to provide a pre-school for African American children, but they lacked the resources. The rationale behind the pre-school program, as Ron Starks claimed, was that black children "get such a bad education in the system . . . But if you get them in those younger years and show them their true identity and the true role of society, they will understand better."[63] The Panthers believed that black children needed to be provided with knowledge of their history and culture so that they would have a greater knowledge of self.

Besides the decentralization plan, the Party also continually served as a watchdog of the Milwaukee Police Department. One illustration of this was their participation in the Committee of 21, a community organization that developed out of the slayings of three African Americans, John Starks, Mary Pendleton, and Jerry Brookshire. As a part of this Committee, the Panthers demanded an investigation and an indictment of Milwaukee police officers for the killings of John Starks and Mary Pendleton in the winter of 1974. Starks was killed by a bullet from the police and Pendleton died from smoke inhalation from tear gas that officers shot into the apartment that the two shared. The police stated that they were looking for a murderer and they mistook Starks as the killer. Despite the efforts of the Panthers and the Committee, a jury once again ruled that the killings were justifiable homicide.[64]

The Milwaukee Black Panthers and the Committee of 21 also demanded an indictment of police officer Raymond Marlow, who was suspected of murdering sixteen-year-old Jerry Brookshire. Marlow maintained that he accidentally shot Brookshire on December 24, 1974. Officer Marlow stated that he had his gun cocked while he and another officer attempted to place the youth in the "spread-eagle position." While doing the procedure, Marlow claimed that Brookshire resisted arrest, causing Marlow to fall and the gun to discharge.[65]

In addition to Marlow's highly dubious story, a local African American, Ola Mae Davis, testified that she saw Marlow deliberately shoot Brookshire while the boy was attempting to scale a fence. As a result of her testimony, Davis had her house firebombed, along with the motel she moved into, and she also received countless threatening phone calls. The Panthers reacted to the situation by staging a major rally in August of 1975 to create greater awareness in the community about this case. Marlow received only a slight reprimand, however, from a coroner's jury who ruled his actions negligent and not criminal.[66]

The Milwaukee branch of the Black Panther Party took part in almost every worthwhile community project they could. For instance, in April of 1975, the Milwaukee Black Panthers joined in a coalition of Milwaukee organizations, including Project Involve (a senior citizen's group), Women United for Action, and U.S. Steelworkers, in their denunciation of a proposed hike in bus fares. As of April of 1975, bus fares in Milwaukee were already at a national high of 60 cents. The proposal was slated to raise fares to seventy-five cents, which would have been one of the highest bus fares in the world. The Black Panthers assisted in drafting a proposal that called for free bus service, with banks and large corporations paying the cost to run the buses. The Party rationalized that the wealthy businesses should pay for the service because they needed those workers who rode the bus. Furthermore, the Panthers were also active in June of 1975 during the Milwaukee meatcutter's strike, where the predominantly black Local 248 protested their wages of $1.39 an hour. [67]

In addition, the Panthers mounted active opposition to U.S. Senate Bill number 1 in April of 1975. This proposed piece of legislation was known as the Criminal Justice Reform Act of 1975, which would have severely curtailed the rights of many United States' citizens. The Bill was labeled by its critics as "the most repressive piece of legislation since the days of the Alien and Sedition laws."[68] Among some of its measures, Senate Bill 1 would have made executions mandatory for certain criminal offenses and the Bill also called for fifteen years imprisonment, or a $100,000 fine, for membership in an organization that called for revolutionary change.[69] According to the *Milwaukee Star-Times*, Senate Bill 1 sought to extend:

> . . . government's power over individuals. This extension can take the form of wiretapping and other secret surveillance, of giving broad discretion to officials in decision about punishment, of authorizing exceptionally severe sentences, or restricting access to critical info about government operations.[70]

The Panthers exerted considerable political pressure on Wisconsin Senators William Proxmire and Gaylord Nelson, as well as Representative Henry Reuss, which helped to draw much needed attention towards defeating the Bill. The Party did not play a pivotal role in the destruction of Senate Bill 1, which died on the floor of the United State's Senate in 1976, but they played a part nonetheless.[71]

The Panthers also spent a great deal of effort combating the use of the "Death Chambers" at Waupun State Prison in Wisconsin. The Death Chambers were soundproof isolation cells, described as "screamers," located in the basement of Waupun Prison. The inmates knew these cells would be used to break prison inmates who were deemed unruly.[72] In June of 1976, the Panthers started their campaign against the Death Chambers by collecting over 3,000 signatures protesting their use. The Milwaukee Panthers also staged a rally on July 27 in Milwaukee, where the editor-in-chief of *The Black Panther* David Dubois was the keynote speaker. By late July of 1976, the Panthers had collected 10,000 signatures from the community.[73] Because the Panthers had mobilized public opinion on the subject, Wisconsin Governor Pat Lucey was forced to order that the cells closed until proven "necessary and humane."[74]

As of March of 1974, the community programs of the Milwaukee branch served roughly 500 people a week. The Panthers supported these programs through a variety of ways. Obtaining financial backing for their programs was not an easy task, and a number of scholars allege that the Black Panther Party, including the Milwaukee branch, used strong-arm tactics to obtain money.[75] The Milwaukee Panthers, like Panthers nation-wide, claimed they did nothing of the sort.[76] In fact, the *Milwaukee Courier* noted that the Panthers "dig into their own pockets to . . . support the survival (community) programs."[77] Michael McGee also claimed that many employed Panther members contributed roughly 40 to 50 percent of their salaries to the Party so that the community programs could function ade-quately.[78] Not only did individual Party members donate large sums of their salary to the Party, the Panthers also attempted to save money by renting poorly maintained, low-rent properties, for their headquarters, which fre-quently doubled as their living quarters. For instance, the Panther's March 1974 headquarters, on 2470 North 3rd Street, was essentially a "collaps-ing" storefront.[79] Also, Panthers often times lived eight or nine to a house so that they could pool their resources and reduce the amount of money spent on rent.[80]

Michael McGee stated, that as a Panther, "You had to humble your-self a lot," because not only did Panthers have to go without basic comforts, many Milwaukee Panthers had to beg to raise money for their community programs.[81] McGee estimated that some Panthers raised $300 a day beg-ging, or "canning," as it was called. Canning was an essential element to the Party's survival, therefore, roughly five to six Panthers canned everyday.[82]

In addition to canning in Milwaukee, the Milwaukee Panthers also went to Madison on occasion, to solicit donations from sympathetic stu-dents at the University of Wisconsin-Madison, after the students had received their financial aid for the semester. The Party found the trips to Madison quite lucrative and reportedly raised as much as $2,000 per trip.[83]

The Milwaukee Panthers also picketed large merchants, like Kohl's, and I & L grocery stores, for money and food donations for their pro-grams.[84] In addition, the Panthers participated in rallies, such as one spon-sored by Students for a Democratic Society in September of 1969, in order to raise funds for their programs in addition to bail money.[85] Furthermore, each Panther member reportedly needed to sell roughly 100 papers weekly in order to keep the Milwaukee branch afloat financially.[86] The Party also held benefits, such as the showing of the "The Cage," a play about oppressive prison life, in July of 1976.[87]

The multitude of programs and services provided by the Milwaukee Panthers clearly illustrate the Party's commitment to helping Milwaukee's lower-income and working-class African American community. Regardless of the need for, and notoriety of these other community services, however, no program could match the impact and legacy of the Breakfast for Children Program.

Chapter Five
Leading by Example

Hunger was, and unfortunately remains, a very real threat for many citizens of Milwaukee, including thousands of children. Therefore, during the late 1960s and early 1970s, the Milwaukee Black Panthers attempted to meet the needs of the lower-income populace of Milwaukee by establishing a Breakfast for Children Program. The Milwaukee Panthers stated, "None of our people . . . if we can help it, will have to beg for food to eat."[1] The Panther's Breakfast Program was a much needed service not only because it combated childhood hunger in Milwaukee, but also because of the positive effects that it had on a child's school attendance, alertness, and ability and desire to learn. For example, the Social Development Commission of Milwaukee noted that hungry children were twelve times as likely to suffer from dizziness, four times as likely to suffer from fatigue and three times as likely to be irritable, making the learning process very difficult for the child.[2] The 1993 Annual Report of the Hunger Task Force of Milwaukee also supported the hypothesis of the Social Development Commission. The Report states:

> It has been documented that children who participate in school breakfast programs are more alert and more able to concentrate, are less often absent or late for school, show greater improvement in standardized tests and in general, have a better attitude toward school.[3]

Given widespread knowledge of the detrimental effects of hunger on a child's ability to function, the Panthers could not fathom why the Milwaukee Public School (MPS) system did not have a breakfast program. The federal government, in fact, created a nationwide breakfast program in 1966, that offered substantial federal funding for local communities offering breakfast programs. As of 1969, however, the Milwaukee school system had "refused to take part in the federally financed free breakfast program."[4] As a result, the Panthers were highly "critical of the Milwaukee School System for not providing" a breakfast program.[5] Dakin Gentry, of the Milwaukee branch, stated that "the schools and the board of education should have had this program instituted a long time ago. It is very difficult for our children to learn anything when they have empty stomachs."[6]

Nevertheless, the Milwaukee School Board seemed uninterested in the plight of inner city, predominantly black children, and bristled at the thought of giving "handouts." Moreover, the Milwaukee School Board refused to implement a free breakfast program because the city of Milwaukee would have to fund a small portion of the program.[7] Therefore, the Milwaukee Panthers believed they had to set the example for the Milwaukee School Board and the city of Milwaukee by establishing a breakfast program of their own.

In May of 1969, the Milwaukee Panthers began publicizing their proposed Breakfast Program in order to generate community awareness as well as to obtain funding for it. In a 1969 newsletter from the Milwaukee Black Panthers, the Party stated:

> The Black Panther Party is the *People's Party*. We will respond to the needs of the people. We are requesting churches, stores, businesses and individuals for space, food and money donations to feed some hungry children. We do not ask that you believe in our philosophy—just to help feed hungry children.[8]

Following the distribution of the newsletter, the Party held a rally at St. Boniface in May of 1969 as part of their efforts to draw attention to the Breakfast Program.[9] At the rally, the Panthers announced that their Breakfast Program would be a free program for schoolchildren, "both black and white."[10] In addition, the Panthers participated in a panel discussion on the Party, at the UWM Student Union in May, in order to draw further attention to the Breakfast Program, as well as to the Party as a whole. At the UWM Student Union, the Party pleaded for volunteers to help run the Breakfast Program.[11] The Panthers asked for help from the community not only because the Party needed the extra help and resources, but also because the Party wanted the larger community to play an active role in providing for its citizens as well. In addition to the rally and panel discussion, the Panthers also brought David Hilliard, National Chief of Staff of the Panthers, to Milwaukee to speak at another rally in order to create additional support and funding for the Breakfast Program.[12]

The Panthers held one last rally on June 7th at Cross Lutheran Church's Youth Center, also known as the "Soul Hole," to further advertise their Breakfast Program. [13] At the Soul Hole rally, Paul Crayton, Lieutenant of Religion of the Milwaukee Panthers and former intern pastor at Cross Lutheran, remarked, "It will be a free breakfast program for children, but if a few of you older people get hungry, just drop in too. We'll feed you too." [14] Crayton also solidified the previously mentioned concerns of the Social Development Commission when he stated, "the main purpose of the (Breakfast) program is to feed kids in the community that are hungry. Many times kids go to school hungry and they can't function like they want to." [15]

Shortly after the fundraiser at the Soul Hole, the Panthers met with the Rev. Joseph Ellwanger from Cross Lutheran, a church with 400 members, roughly 40 percent of whom were black, to ask permission to run the Breakfast Program out of the Soul Hole. Ellwanger tentatively approved the idea, but said he would have to consult with Cross Lutheran's church council. In the meantime, the Panthers thought they had an agreement with Cross Lutheran, and they distributed fliers stating the program would be held at the Church. However, the Church Council of Cross Lutheran, an interracial body of the Church's leaders, ruled that it would not allow this controversial black militant group to use its facilities regardless of their good intentions.[16] Ellwanger issued a press release stating that the Church could not work "with an organization openly encouraging the violent overthrow of the government and thus violence against people."[17] Furthermore, Ellwanger claimed that the church did not want to give the impression that Cross Lutheran agreed with the militant teachings of the Party.[18] Ellwanger, however, also stated that the church "recognized they (Panthers) were attempting to fill a need."[19] In addition, "Ellwanger said the council did not feel the Panthers' breakfast program was bad but that the children's needs could be better met by the federally financed program."[20]

As a result of the untimely falling out with Cross Lutheran, the Panthers were forced to operate the Breakfast Program out of the home of Paul Crayton, at 1728 North 16th Street. [21] Crayton recognized the poor situation and even called the Panther's facilities "inadequate."[22] Despite the lack of physical space for the Breakfast Program, it was still well attended by the black community, as roughly 100 children attended on a daily basis. Initially, the children were served between 7 and 9 am in rotating shifts of 30. Those who took advantage of the Breakfast Program ranged in age from infants to teenagers, and were predominantly African American. [23] Participants in the Breakfast Program found "plentiful helpings," of pancakes, sausages, oranges and milk. [24] Unfortunately, the Panther's Breakfast Program, at least initially, appeared to adhere to prevailing gender norms of the era, as wives of three Panthers did the cooking, and a handful of teen-aged girls served the food.[25]

The Breakfast Program functioned throughout the summer of 1969, but by mid July, the Panthers reported only feeding 50 to 75 children daily, as opposed to the 100 that they served only a month earlier. The Panthers rationalized that the end of summer school caused the decrease in attendance. The Panthers' Breakfast Program normally ran Monday through Friday, from 7:00 to 9:00 a.m. during school and summer school sessions, but the Panthers changed the hours of operation to 9:00–11:00 a.m., and later to 12:00–2:00 pm, to try and accommodate the summer-time schedules of children. The Breakfast Program, therefore, functioned more as a lunch program during the summer months.[26] Many in the African American community applauded the Panther's efforts. For instance, the *Milwaukee Courier* stated that "the Black Panther Party is to be com-mended for taking the initiative in setting up such a program."[27]

The Panthers sustained the Breakfast Program primarily through previously mentioned fundraising efforts, as well as from contributions from area grocers. [28] For instance, larger grocery chains such as Kohl's and National contributed unspecified amounts to the Party, and locally owned I & L Foods donated $25 worth of food weekly to the Breakfast Program.[29] Altogether, the Panthers reportedly received approximately $500 per week from various Milwaukee grocery stores.[30] As stated in chapter four, however, the Panthers themselves donated their time and money to programs like the Breakfast Program, which accounted for its success. The Breakfast Program of the Milwaukee Panthers, like all of their other programs, ceased operations when the Milwaukee branch was shut down in November of 1969, but the Breakfast Program lived on in other organizations thanks to the Panther's initiative.

Prior to the Panther's Breakfast Program, many Milwaukee com-munity organizations seemed to be dumbfounded that widespread hun-ger existed in Milwaukee. For example, immediately following the disagreement between the Panthers and Cross Lutheran, the Rev. Joseph Ellwanger of Cross Lutheran called for a report from Cross Lutheran's Church Council to determine issues of childhood hunger in Milwaukee.[31] The Church Council deliberated and presented their findings to Ellwanger, who then promptly wrote a letter to countless Milwaukee organizations and churches. The letter stated, "The Church Council of Cross Lutheran Church, in their recent confrontation with the Black Panthers and their breakfast program proposal were brought to a vivid awareness of sev-eral things. That there is a hunger need among Milwaukee children and youth."[32]

Following the report of the Council, Ellwanger and others held a public meeting on July 21st at Cross Lutheran to discuss how to proceed with combating childhood hunger in Milwaukee. At the meeting, the Citizens for Central City School Breakfast Program (CCCSBP) was created. [33] By the end of July, CCCSBP issued a proposal to the Milwaukee School Board calling for a free breakfast program in Milwaukee's schools. The proposal called for breakfast programs in the "inner city, on both the north and south sides, where there are large numbers of children from poor families."[34] The CCCSBP's plan appeared very sound and feasible, thus it was backed by over thirty community groups and churches.[35]

In acknowledging the impetus for the creation of the CCCSBP and its proposed breakfast program, Ellwanger freely admitted that the idea for his program came from the Black Panther Party.[36] Randy Marchese of the CCCSBP supported Ellwanger when he stated, "We are fully willing to endorse the fact that the free breakfast program was initiated by the Panthers." [37]

In formulating their proposal, the CCCSBP studied existing breakfast programs in three Milwaukee parochial schools, as well as those in public schools in St. Paul, Chicago, Cleveland, Flint, Michigan, and Columbus, Ohio. The CCCSBP's studies:

> Concluded that there is a real need for such a nutritional supplement (as provided by a breakfasts program) to the diets of many school children and that such a program has a very positive effect on the behavior patterns, achievement level, and attendance records of nearly all the students involved.[38]

The CCCSBP proposed twelve potential central city schools to house experimental breakfast programs, of which the school board would choose six for the program.[39] The Committee's initial plan stated that it would cost $42,750 to run the breakfast program, and the federal government would cover $25,600 of those expenses. In addition, local organizations and foundations "concerned about the welfare of children" already had pledged an additional $11,000 to support the CCCSBP's plan.[40] Therefore, the School Board only had to allot $6,000 to fund the experimental breakfast program, yet many on the Board still balked at the idea. Apparently the Milwaukee School Board had misplaced priorities, as an editorial in the *Greater Milwaukee Star* noted. The editorial lamented, "Spending thousands of dollars on expensive audio-visual aids and special programs will not help if a child can't attend to the lesson because he is hungry."[41]

The CCCSBP waged a long battle against the intransigent Milwaukee School Board who was committed to not using any tax money for breakfast programs. Those against the breakfast program stated that "it's the parents responsibility" to provide sustenance for their children, and other Board members stated that the main problem was that "some of those welfare mothers are too lazy." [42] Yet others stated, "The purpose of the Milwaukee public schools is primarily, one of education, not, as (School Board) representative Russell Darrow put it, "charity." [43]

Constant pressure by the CCSBP ultimately coerced the Milwaukee School Board to create experimental breakfast programs in three Milwaukee schools in 1970. Approval for the experimental breakfast program was a positive step, although the CCCSBP called for the program to be implemented in fourteen schools as of 1970.[44] Funding concerns continued to be the main impediment to the implementation of a wide-scale breakfast program in Milwaukee.[45] Thomas Farley, Food Services Director for Milwaukee Public Schools, stated that such financial concerns were "unsubstantiated," as breakfasts would not exceed 29.3 cents per meal, of which the Federal Government would pay 15 cents.[46] In 1972, the CCCSBP convinced the School Board to expand the breakfast program to twelve schools. In addition to the locally and federally funded twelve schools, the CCCSBP ran an additional eleven breakfast programs with additional federal funds they had received. All told, these breakfast programs fed over 2,000 children daily.[47]

Also in 1972, The People's Committee for Survival, the forerunner to the second wave of the Milwaukee Panthers, emerged as a community self-help organization in Milwaukee. As part of their community service efforts, the People's Committee launched their Breakfast Program on September 27, 1972, at Elite Church of God and Christ. Less than one year later, the People's Committee became the Black Panther Party of Milwaukee, and the Party formally took over supervision of the Program, now located at a building on 2470 North Third Street. The Panthers were forced to move out of Elite Church of God and Christ because the church raised the rent on the Panther's use of their facilities. The Church mistakenly believed that the Panthers made money on their Breakfast Program, and the Church wanted their share. [48]

At the Panther's Breakfast Program, breakfasts were served between 8:00 and 9:00 a.m., and consisted of eggs, toast, sausage or ham, and orange juice. Like the Panther Breakfast Program of 1969, children did not have to be signed in or registered in order to participate, they simply showed up and were fed. [49]

As with the Panther's Breakfast Program of 1969, the Panther's Breakfast Program of the early 1970s was largely supported by donations from local businesses and individuals. As the *UWM Post Magazine* noted, however, "The Black Panthers receive moral support from the neighborhood but most of the people cannot afford to give financial support."[50] The financial burden of the Breakfast Program was hard for the Panthers to bear as the Program cost the Party roughly $300 a day to feed the children nutritious breakfasts. As Michael McGee stated, "We didn't feed those kids no junk."[51] Panther Roy Maxie, who helped oversee the Breakfast Program, also noted that "the Federal Government with its millions of dollars can't run a decent program," yet the Panthers could with very limited resources.[52] The Panthers made real sacrifices, such as McGee, who woke up at 5:00 am daily, in order to prepare the breakfasts. Some Panthers begged to raise money to fund the program, while in some instances, Panther members pleaded to clerks at grocery stores to sell them food for reduced prices, or give it to the Party free of charge, for the good of the children.[53]

Despite the easy access of the Program and the noble effort of the Panthers, the new Breakfast Program was not as successful as that of the 1969 Milwaukee Panthers. For example, in February of 1973, the People's Committee served less than fifty children a day, and by March of 1974, the Panthers were serving only twenty children daily.[54] The decrease in attendance could largely be explained by the creation of other breakfast programs run by less confrontational organizations, and in the Milwaukee Public Schools, during the Panthers' four-year absence.

The Breakfast Program, and the Party as a whole, lived on for three more years until the Milwaukee Party fragmented, once again, over how to best serve the community, and its members went their separate ways.[55] Even though the Panthers themselves no longer existed as of 1976, their fight for a citywide free breakfast program was carried on by the CCCSBP. In 1974, the five-year old CCCSBP was rewarded for their efforts with funding from the city of Milwaukee for a full-time staff person. Shortly after receiving funding from the City, the CCCSBP changed its name to the Hunger Task Force of Milwaukee (HTFM) in order to illustrate that it was no longer an ad-hoc organization, and to recognize that it was receiving monies from Milwaukee.[56]

In 1975, The Hunger Task Force continued the fight against the lethargic School Board, which persisted in its lack of concern with childhood hunger. Illustrating their lack of concern, School Board member Anthony Bussalachi stated that "the physical neglect of children is not our domain."[57] By 1975, the City of Milwaukee had once again reduced the breakfast programs to three inner city schools. When proponents of a federally funded breakfast program proposed expanding the program to fourteen schools, the Milwaukee School Board went into an uproar. The School Board refused to implement such a program because they thought it would cost more than the Federal Government was willing to reimburse under the Child and Nutrition Act, and the Board would not ask local taxpayers to pay the bill. [58] As the Rev. Ellwanger claimed, the breakfast program would be a reality "if the Board's priorities were less cost-oriented and more people-oriented, particularly poor-oriented."[59] Supporters of the free breakfast program also asked, "If a free breakfast program cannot be worked into a total public school budget of some $245 million, they asked, where are the Board's priorities?"[60]

In addition to the Board's unwillingness to help poor and hungry children, were the now inflated numbers for the breakfast program in 1975, as presented by Tom Farley, Director of Food Services for Milwaukee Public Schools. Farley, who as of 1970, claimed that the program was economically feasible, now estimated that the program would cost sixty-seven cents per meal, or twenty-two cents over the Federal Government's limit for reimbursement. The Hunger Task Force, however, estimated that it would only cost 52 cents per meal. [61] Many individuals in the community were skeptical of Farley's figures, because most cities, including Washington D.C. and Chicago, had no problems staying beneath the Government's financial ceiling. Nevertheless, citing Farley's figures, in November of 1975, the School Board voted 10–5 against expansion of the breakfast program. Opponents of breakfast expansion stated it would cost too much, that children waste much of the food, and that "parents should feed their own kids anyway."[62] Finally, in 1976, Milwaukee Public Schools cut free breakfast programs altogether, and Milwaukee would not see another free school breakfast program until 1980.[63]

As of 1979, Milwaukee remained the only city of the nation's twenty-five largest cities that did not have a breakfast program. Regardless of the setbacks that the Hunger Task Force endured, they relentlessly pushed for a free school breakfast program. In 1979, the Hunger Task Force was rewarded for their efforts with a federal grant that was designed to help them run an experimental breakfast program. As a result of the HTFM's successful program and "enormous community pressure," the HTFM convinced the School Board to implement a free breakfast program in sixteen elementary schools in the city of Milwaukee in 1980. [64] In 1981, the breakfast program spread to forty-nine Milwaukee public schools, and by 1987, nine thousand children were being fed at free school breakfast programs.[65]

Besides the much needed breakfast program, the Hunger Task Force of Milwaukee provided many other services to the city. For instance, in 1982 the HTFM began operating the Emergency Food Pantry Network in Milwaukee. By 1987, the Food Pantry Network reached 30,000 people every month, and by 1990, the Pantry served 19,000 children every month. In

1993, HTFM provided the 125 food pantries in Milwaukee with 70 tons of food, which was enough to feed 38,000 people a month, 25,000 of whom were children. By 1997, the Hunger Task Force fed 44,000 people monthly, roughly half being children.[66] As of 2003, the Task Force fed 45,000 people monthly at its various pantries, and yet another 60,000 at its homeless shelters.[67] Granted, the Milwaukee Black Panthers never worked directly with the Hunger Task Force, but the history of HTFM, especially its origins, cannot be separated from the history of the Panthers.

In conclusion, the Panther's Breakfast Program was a success. The Program was a triumph because the Party galvanized the larger Milwaukee community into action on the issue of childhood hunger, and that was the main goal of the Breakfast Program. As Panther Walter Chesser stated in May of 1969, the "community will hopefully take it (the Program) over."[68] Later in June of 1969, the Panthers also noted that they "hoped to turn the program over to private groups after first showing how it could be done."[69] The Party knew they did not have the widespread appeal or the resources to adequately serve the Milwaukee community on a prolonged basis, nor was that their purpose. In addition, the Panthers knew there were other pressing issues besides hunger, such as police brutality and lack of accessible health care for the poor, that they had to address. [70] In providing the spark, the Panthers hoped that they could instigate social change that would outlive their organizational existence, and that is what they accomplished with their Breakfast Program.

Chapter Six
Romanticizing the Past?

Countless works dealing with the Black Panther Party have solely focused on the Party's flaws, or at the very least, have distorted its failings.[1] In contrast, *The Black Panthers in the Midwest* has offered a reassessment of the Black Panther Party through an extensive examination of the numerous social services and programs that the Party provided. The Party, and specifically, the Milwaukee branch, did have its share of faults and problems, however. Therefore, chapter six analyzes the shortcomings of the Milwaukee branch in order to present a more well-rounded analysis of the Black Panther Party so that the Milwaukee Panthers are not romanticized.

Even though police persecution was the primary reason why the first wave of the Milwaukee Panthers disbanded, internal dissension also helped to pull the branch apart. For example, in November of 1969, shortly after the trial of the Milwaukee Three concluded, Dakin Gentry requested that the Central Committee, the Party's national decision-making committee, disband the local branch for what Gentry perceived as lack of success in the community.[2] Many Panthers, such as Lovetta X and the Milwaukee Three, were outraged because Gentry never showed the letter to the Panther rank-and-file, nor consulted with them before making such an important, yet arbitrary decision.[3]

Shortly after Gentry issued the press release calling for the dissolution of the Milwaukee branch, the Milwaukee Three verbally attacked Gentry in the *Milwaukee Courier*. To the Milwaukee Three, Gentry's decision to ask for the Central Committee to disband the Milwaukee branch reeked of sabotage. One of the Three, Jesse White, went so far as to call Gentry a "pig' just doing your job like a good boy."[4] The Three also maintained that Gentry was to blame for many of the shortcomings of the Milwaukee branch. In addition, the Milwaukee Three claimed that the Party was entirely centered around Gentry and Felix Welch, and that they neglected the concerns and contributions of the general Panther membership.[5]

The Milwaukee Three further claimed that Gentry and Nate Bellamy had "sold-out." To substantiate their claim, the Three pointed to the jobs that Gentry and Bellamy had within the City's "Concentrated Employment Office" less than a month after resigning from the Party.[6] Joe McClain, formerly of the NAACP Commandos, supported this assertion by stating that the local government in Milwaukee frequently offered various social service jobs to black militants of the era. For instance, a number of Youth Commandos took jobs working for the City, where they served the people in drug or prison rehab projects. The problem, according to McClain, however, was that the former Commandos now had their militancy stifled because they now had to work within the confines of a bureaucracy.[7]

The Milwaukee Three also maintained that Gentry took the job with the City to avoid going to jail, as was the inevitable course for many Panther leaders throughout the country.[8] Furthermore, the Three alleged that Gentry stepped down from his position within the Party simply because he was beaten by the police.[9] As Jesse White, one of the Milwaukee Three, said, "When the struggle really gets tough you'll find out who's just there to find out what was going down," and who was actually committed to the cause.[10]

Lovetta X supported the claims of the Milwaukee Three in a separate interview in the *Milwaukee Courier* in January of 1970. Lovetta stated that those in leadership positions within the Milwaukee branch, such as Bellamy and Gentry, "contained and controlled the rest of the members of the party under their bullshit methods, like psyching people through the forceful manner that they had."[11] Lovetta also claimed that Dakin Gentry hurt the Party, and the black community of Milwaukee as a whole, when he stated on local television that the "people in Milwaukee were forming guerilla bands to counteract what the police are doing in the community."[12] Lovetta X maintained that it was highly destructive to say something as inflammatory and incorrect as what Gentry said. She also said his statement could potentially cause the Milwaukee police to become even more repressive towards the black community in an effort to sift out these fictitious "guerilla bands."[13] Furthermore, it is arguable that Gentry further alienated the rank-and-file by not attempting to bail out four Panthers who had been jailed for carrying concealed weapons in June of 1969.[14]

Gentry eventually retaliated to the aforementioned criticisms in another interview in the *Milwaukee Courier*. Gentry reasserted that he resigned from the Party, and asked that the branch be dissolved because he did not think that he, nor the Panthers, were serving the people properly.[15] Gentry's short rebuttal ended by labeling the critiques on his character and decisions as nothing more than "bullshit."[16]

Not only did Gentry apparently cause fissures within the Party, he also hindered the Panther's ability to serve the people by preventing alliances with some other progressive organizations. For instance, Joe McClain, stated that when the Panthers became established in Milwaukee in 1969, that Dakin Gentry visited the Commandos to inform them that the Panthers were "taking over" the movement.[17] McClain, on the other hand, did not see why there was not enough room for both groups, as well as others, in the struggle. McClain and other Commandos were not very enthusiastic about working with the Panthers after Gentry's brash statement, however.[18] In addition, according to FBI documents, the Panthers "invaded" a Commando meeting on May 10, 1969 at St. Boniface to further reiterate that the Panthers "were now in charge."[19]

The Milwaukee Three, Lovetta X and Joe McClain were not the only ones to place blame on the Party itself for its dissolution either. Ronald Starks, member of both waves of the Black Panther Party in Milwaukee, called Walter Chesser, former Deputy Minister of Defense of the 1969 Panthers, an opportunist who was highly detrimental to the Milwaukee branch. Following Starks comments, Chesser demanded an apology from Starks and challenged him to a debate, which Starks declined.[20] FBI records also reveal other internal problems in Milwaukee by May of 1969. For instance, an unnamed individual who handled publication and distribution of the Black Panther newsletter for the Milwaukee branch, was purged by local leadership.[21]

In addition, it appears as if the Milwaukee branch over-disciplined some of their troublemakers on occasion. According to FBI documents, the Milwaukee branch had a "People's Jail" located in the basement of their headquarters on 2121 North 1st Street, where they placed those who violated various Party rules (See Appendix B). The "jail" had no toilet, and "inmates" were not provided any food. One unnamed Panther was imprisoned in the "jail" for disappearing for nine days, then reappearing in a tavern proclaiming that he was the leader of the Black Panther Party. When representatives of the Milwaukee branch informed the national leadership of their situation, the national leadership told them to release their "prisoner," and purge him from the Party.[22]

In addition to the previously mentioned internal conflicts with the Milwaukee branch, the Black Panther Party's militant image also attracted the wrong people to the Party. According to Gentry, some individuals wanted to join the Party because they viewed the Panthers as a "gun club or some sort of guerilla outfit." [23] Gentry stated that when the uniformed prospective members "learned that the party required discipline (see Appendix B), study and hard work in political action, some changed their minds about joining."[24] Lovetta X substantiated Gentry's point when she claimed that some people joined the Milwaukee branch simply because it was a power-trip and trendy, not because they seriously cared about the community.[25] Non-committed Panthers, as described by Lovetta X, did not want to work in the community programs, or help with the day-to-day operations of the Black Panther Party. Therefore, tensions arose between those Panthers devoted to helping the community, and those who only cared about being chic.[26]

Furthermore, the Party had to deal with problems resulting largely from espousing atheist, communistic ideas, during the Cold War years, to a religious, politically unaware, lower-income African American community.[27] The Milwaukee Panthers realized, however, that many in the black community of Milwaukee did not want to have anything to do with an organization that hinted of communism. [28] Joe McClain supported the Panther's views of the African American community, as he claimed that the Panther's revolutionary and communistic rhetoric could not reach the relatively uniformed working-class black masses.[29] As a result of the aversion of many Milwaukee African Americans to communist teachings, some Panthers, such as Abdullah Salahadyn, went out of their way to assure the community that the Party was not a communist organization. Despite Salahadyn's claims however, the Black Panther Party, including the Milwaukee branch, frequently taught from the *Red Book*, as well as other communist writings, thus hurting their efforts to reach the black community in Milwaukee.[30]

The 1969 Panthers also had serious difficulties working with other community organizations and churches, as illustrated by the disagreement with Cross Lutheran Church over the Panther's Breakfast Program.[31] After the Panthers and Cross Lutheran had their falling out, the Panthers claimed that Cross Lutheran had "no interest in serving hungry children." [32] Furthermore, the Information Staff of the Milwaukee branch submitted an article to the Party's national newsletter, the *Black Panther*, which called the Rev. Joseph Ellwanger a "punk racist, fascist pig preacher."[33] First, if Cross Lutheran and Ellwanger had no interest in stopping hunger, they would not have helped create the Citizens for Central City School Breakfast Program (CCCSBP) nor the Hunger Task Force of Milwaukee (HTFM). Second, Ellwanger would not have preached at Cross Lutheran, with a membership that was 40 percent African American, if he was racist. Finally, Ellwanger would not have created CCCSBP or HTFM, organizations that predominantly served poor blacks, if he was bigoted.

In addition to the spat with Cross Lutheran, the Panthers also had an issue with Milwaukee's St. Mark's AME Church. At a Sunday church service in early August of 1969, Lovetta X and Will Crittenden, Director of the Black Arts Theater in Milwaukee, interrupted a church service at St. Marks AME Church to demand that the church allow its facilities to be used for Black Arts performances.[34] Based on their run-ins with the Commandos and St. Mark's, it appears that the Party wanted to dictate their agenda to other, more established institutions, in the community. Such behavior did not bode well for garnering support in the Milwaukee black community.

The Milwaukee branch, like many Panther branches throughout the nation, was also accused of indoctrinating young children in their Breakfast Program.[35] The alleged indoctrination of children was one of the reasons why Ellwanger and Cross Lutheran voted not to have the Breakfast Program at the Church.[36] At the Breakfast Program, the Panthers shouted revolutionary slogans and chants that were viewed by many as not appropriate for children. For example, the Milwaukee Panthers encouraged the children to "take from the greedy and give to the needy."[37] In essence, it could be argued that the Panthers were telling young children with formative minds that it was okay to steal.

The 1969 Panthers were also guilty of making a number of other uniformed statements that damaged the credibility and purpose of the organization. For example, Panther John Trenton made the widespread generalization that middle-class blacks were "house niggers," or subservient to whites, while the Panthers were "field niggers," or in other words, militants.[38] An African American organization dedicated to positive social change does not need to refer to itself in such pejorative terms. In addition, Trenton's statement possibly alienated potential allies in the middle-class African American community. Furthermore, Trenton's comment illustrated his general lack of knowledge of the Party, as the Panthers had numerous middle-class members and supporters.[39]

Lovetta X also made a fatal mistake, a-la the Beatles, when she likened the persecution of the Black Panther Party to that of Jesus Christ.[40] As Lovetta said, "Jesus was a threat to the government in those days and was arrested just like revolutionaries are today; just like Huey P. Newton."[41] The religious, lower-income Milwaukee black populace probably did not appreciate having Newton compared to Christ in any fashion.

The 1973 Black Panthers also had their share of flaws, or at least actions that could be perceived as flaws, as well. For example, members of the Milwaukee branch frequently "liberated" items for use in their community programs, especially the Breakfast for Children Program.[42] As Mike McGee stated, that despite the fundraising efforts, the Party "couldn't raise enough money" for the Breakfast Program. Therefore the Panthers believed they had to steal to provide for the Breakfast Program.[43] McGee claimed, understandably, that he and other Panthers would much rather steal, than tell hungry children that there was not any food for them. McGee also maintained that the Party did not steal from any small, independently owned grocery stores, but only from the larger chain stores.[44]

In addition, the 1973 Panthers had to contend with internal problems as well. For instance, Michael McGee, an individual who had helped re-establish the Party in Milwaukee, was expelled from the Panthers in 1974. Apparently, McGee had acted alone and without the Party's authorization, when he filed a suit against the Milwaukee Police Department requesting the Red Squad's secret files.[45] As a result of this seemingly minor action on the part of McGee, he was denounced by others within the Milwaukee branch for "very questionable and devious activities," and forced to leave the Panthers by 1974.[46]

A factor that possibly contributed to McGee's dismissal, as well as a further illustration of internal problems with the Party, was his decision to place women within positions of leadership in the Party. According to Michael McGee, "Women carried 60 percent of the load," of the Black Panther Party in Milwaukee.[47] Despite the fact that Panther women, such as Doris Brown, played a pivotal role in the Milwaukee branch, numerous Party males refused to acknowledge their contributions or role within the Party. McGee reported that he had to suspend certain males, as well as expel males on occasion, for their blatantly sexist behavior. McGee was called a "wimp" or a "fag" by sexist males who resented his ideas about gender equality.[48] It is very likely that McGee's gender neutral policies hastened his removal from the Party.

Chapter six addressed the handfuls of failings, or perceived failings, of the Black Panther Party in Milwaukee, in order to present a more complete story about the Party. As chapter six illustrates, the Party did have its share of flaws, but as Lovetta X stated, "a majority of the Panthers were for real. They wanted to work and they did work."[49] To exclusively focus on the shortcomings of a select minority of the Party would be a detriment to the Milwaukee branch, and to our overall understanding of this Black Power organization.

Conclusion

The Black Panther Party of Milwaukee shared many characteristics with other Panther branches throughout the nation, but it did have some unique qualities of its own. In order to illustrate that the Milwaukee Panthers were not a complete aberration from other Panther branches throughout the nation, the conclusion will briefly examine similarities, as well as the differences that the Black Panther Party had with other Panther branches.

Like other Panther branches around the country, the Milwaukee Panthers armed themselves. Yet, the Milwaukee branch did not place much emphasis on guns, but rather on carrying out community programs. Countless newspaper articles can be found in the *Milwaukee Courier, Greater Milwaukee Star, Milwaukee Journal* and *Milwaukee Sentinel*, that address the Panther's community programs in some fashion, yet hardly any articles ever mention the Panther's weaponry. In fact, only one newspaper article, the June 12th, 1969 edition of the *Milwaukee Sentinel*, devoted significant attention to the weaponry of the Milwaukee Panthers.[1] If the Panthers had placed high priority on carrying guns, the largely conservative, mainstream Milwaukee news media would have surely mentioned it as frequently as possible in order to portray the Panthers as a dangerous, neo-terrorist organization.

A relatively unique feature of the Milwaukee Party is that no Milwaukee Panther was ever killed by the police, which is not something that all other branches and chapters could claim. The lack of death among the Milwaukee branch is fairly remarkable considering the brutality of the Milwaukee Police Department. One plausible explanation is the police never had to resort to deadly force in Milwaukee because the first wave of the Panthers were repressed so quickly through jailings and beatings. And when the Panthers re-emerged in 1973, the Black Panther Party as a whole had de-emphasized the guns to such an extent that the police did not feel

the need to exterminate what they perceived to be a non-threatening organization.

One other rather distinctive quality of the 1969 Milwaukee Panthers
is that they were disbanded by the Party's Central Committee after only
eleven months. Other Panther branches dealt with significant purges, but
very few were completely disbanded. The Milwaukee Panthers were also
unique in that they were re-established, which to this author's knowledge,
happened only to the Los Angeles branch.

As already noted in chapters two and six, conflict within the Milwaukee branch, and within Panther ranks as a whole, was fairly commonplace.
The amount of dissension and purging that occurred throughout Panther
chapters and branches may raise some doubts about the commitment and
dependability of Fanon's lumpenproletariat.[2] Some scholars, such as Chris
Booker, claim that the Panthers' "emphasis on the lumpen was a decisive
factor in the Black Panther Party's eventual decline."[3] Before a broad generalization such as Booker's can be made it is important to remember that
predominantly middle-class organizations, such as SNCC and the NAACP,
experienced great rifts. In addition to SNCC's highly publicized dismissal of
whites from the organization in 1966, there also were day-to-day problems
among the leaders of the organization. The NAACP also had trouble with
branches and individuals, such as Robert F. Williams, who differed with
their tactics. In addition, the NAACP routinely had problems between the
older members and the Youth Councils, something that was especially visible in Milwaukee.[4] When it is further noted that the Panthers were prime
targets of federal and local enforcement agencies that instilled general sus-
picion and paranoia among many Panthers, it becomes somewhat under-
standable why the Panthers expelled countless members throughout its
existence. There also is the general question of how prevalent the lumpen
were within the Party. Charles Jones notes that although Seale and Newton
placed great emphasis on recruiting the lumpen, "the socioeconomic profile of the rank-and-file Panthers contradicts the lumpen perception of the
organization."[5]

Finally, one of the clearest similarities between the Milwaukee
branch and other Panther branches, was the priority they placed on
serving lower-income African American communities. The Milwaukee
Panthers provided a host of community programs and services, and as
Appendix E illustrates, the Milwaukee branch was not alone in providing
various self-help programs. Panther branches across the nation dedicated
themselves to serving segments of the black community. As Miriam White
noted in her Master's Thesis from the University of Wisconsin-Madison,
"While it was the gun-toting militant black man and woman that was

their (Panthers) most publicized image, in reality, the Black Panthers devoted nearly all their energies to constructing and carrying out social programs."[6] As a result of the Panther's commitment to the community, the Party received quite a bit of support from the lower-income African American community, who, "though they did not actively or financially support the BPP, went home to sit on the corner, where manhood is not so costly, and applaud those 'little angry niggers' who weren't gonna take it no more."[7]

In closing, the community programs defined the Black Panther Party as an organization. Any examination of the Black Panthers that does not adequately address the importance of the community programs is neglecting one of the most tangible and enduring legacies of this controversial Black Power organization.

Epilogue

It would be nice to think that issues such as police brutality and hunger are not as prevalent in Milwaukee as they were in the 1960s and 1970s. Some progress has been made, as Harold Breier's racist administration is long gone. In addition, Arthur Jones, an African American, was Police Chief during the late 1990s and early 2000s, and David Clarke, also an African American, is currently the Sheriff of Milwaukee County. Furthermore, Nannette (Nan) Hegerty, a white woman, is now the Chief of Police. Regardless of the diversity in the leadership within the City's and County's police forces, it does not appear, however, that the Milwaukee Police Department of the 1990s and 2000's is vastly different than that of the Police Department of the 1960s and 1970s. For instance, there have been numerous instances of police brutality against the African American and Latino communities of Milwaukee over the past few years.

One such example of police violence was the killing of Antonio Davis. Davis, an African American, was killed by a Milwaukee Police Officer, Byron Andrews, in 1998. Andrews maintained that Davis tried to run him down with a car. As a result, Andrews claimed that he drew his gun and pointed it at Davis on purpose, but that he fired it accidentally.[1] A number of witnesses disputed Andrews' account, yet at the official inquest, jurors ruled the death an accident, but claimed that there had been "severe negligence on the part of Officer Byron Andrews."[2]

Another instance of police brutality occurred in the Fall of 2002, and this incident was caught on tape by cameras in a Milwaukee jail. The local news showed the footage of an African American male being accosted by a brutish white male police officer, Robert Henry, in the jail. After the incident was over, Henry gloated over his "accomplishment" by flexing his massive arms. Soon after the incident was over, Arthur Jones fired Henry, but then Henry filed a $300,000 reverse discrimination suit against the

City. In the suit, Henry claimed that two African American officers should have been disciplined as well, but were not because they were black. As a result, Milwaukee's Police and Fire Commission overturned Henry's firing. Worse yet, Henry applied for disability in 2003, as he claimed that he suffered severe mental stress from the whole ordeal. In June of 2003, Henry was granted lifetime disability, and allotted roughly $40,000 a year for the next 29 years. Henry now lives in Florida.[3]

Also in the Fall of 2002, Larry Jenkins, an African American, was shot by Milwaukee Police Officer John Bartlett.[4] Jenkins was not carrying a weapon when he was shot. The shooting was ruled "justifiable," and Bartlett was not disciplined.[5] In addition, Samuel Rodriquez, a Latino, was also shot and killed by Milwaukee Police, and once again, the suspect was unarmed when shot.[6]

Another case of police brutality occurred in the Fall of 2004, when Frank Jude, Jr., an African American male, was severely beaten by off-duty police officers. Jude had accompanied two white women to a party at one of the officer's homes, and was accused of stealing an officer's badge, and then beaten. Jude maintained that he did not steal anything, and that numerous racial epithets were hurled at him before he was beaten.[7] Especially disturbing, is that Officer John Bartlett was also involved in this incident.[8] Bartlett, along with twelve others, were eventually fired, or at least disciplined.[9]

In the Spring of 2005, Wilbert Prado, a Latino, was shot and killed by Alfonzo Glover, an off-duty police officer. According to Glover, he had allegedly been followed by Prado in his van. Glover got out of his car to confront Prado, who supposedly hit Glover with the van. Glover fired at Prado as a result, hitting the van ten times. Apparently, a foot chase ensued, which resulted in Glover shooting Prado eight times. No weapon was found on Prado.[10] Eugene Kane, a columnist for the *Milwaukee Journal Sentinel*, wrote, "When you consider that Prado was apparently killed while fleeing the scene, it's hard to figure out exactly why this cop felt his life was in such danger he had to rain down a storm of gunfire on an unarmed suspect."[11]

In addition to the issue of police brutality, hunger remains a severe problem for many lower-income Milwaukee residents. In 1999, on the first day of Summerfest, a yearly music, food and beer festival held in Milwaukee, I ventured down to the Festival and I saw firsthand the legacy of the Milwaukee Black Panther Party, as well as the depressing situation that still exists in the City. Over 100 Hunger Task Force volunteers collected more than 30,000 pounds of food from 14,000 Summerfest goers on this day alone as a part of the HTFM's continual battle with hunger.[12] The HTFM is also still engaging in a constant battle with local and state politicians to improve the breakfast programs in our Wisconsin schools. As of 2003, however, Wisconsin ranked last in the nation in terms of school participation in free breakfast programs.[13]

As Wisconsin citizens, as well as the rest of the nation, continue to become more conservative it is doubtful that issues like police brutality or hunger will noticeably improve. Our nation's priorities are skewed as we prioritize obtaining oil in foreign countries over providing basic human necessities for our fellow Americans. If we continue to neglect our nation's poor and downtrodden, hopefully another Black Panther Party-type organization will emerge in the United States. The group might be comprised of poor Appalachian whites, or of migrant workers, or lower-income African Americans in urban areas. And once again, they will state:

> We hold these truths to be self-evident, that all men are created equal; that they are endowed by their Creator with certain unalienable rights; that among these are life, liberty, and the pursuit of happiness. That, to secure these rights, governments are instituted among men, deriving their just powers from the consent of the governed; that, whenever any form of government becomes destructive to these ends, it is the right of the people to alter or abolish it, and to institute a new government, laying its foundation on such principles, and organizing its powers in such form, as to them shall seem most likely to effect their safety and happiness.

Appendix A
The 10-Point Program of the Black Panther Party

1. We want freedom. We want power to determine the destiny of our Black Community.

    We believe that black people will not be free until we are able to determine our destiny.

2. We want full employment for our people.

    We believe that the federal government is responsible and obligated to give every man employment or a guaranteed income. We believe that if the white American businessmen will not give full employment, then the means of production should be taken from the businessmen and placed in the community so that the people of the community can organize and employ all of its people and give a high standard of living.

3. We want an end to the robbery by the CAPITALIST man of our Black Community.

    We believe that this racist government has robbed us and now we are demanding the overdue debt of forty acres and two mules. Forty acres and two mules was promised 100 years ago as restitution for slave labor and mass murder of black people. We will accept the payment in currency which will be distributed to our many communities. The Germans are now aiding the Jews in Israel for the genocide of the Jewish people. The Germans killed six million Jews. The American racist has taken part in the slaughter of over fifty million black people; therefore, we feel that this is a modest demand that we make.

4. We want decent housing, fit for shelter of human beings.

    We believe that if the white landlords will not give decent housing to our black community, then the housing and the land should be made into cooperatives so that our community, with government aid, can build and make decent housing for its people.

5. We want education for our people that exposes the true nature of this decadent American society. We want education that teaches us our true history and our role in the present-day society.

    We believe in an educational system that will give to our people a knowledge of self. If a man does not have knowledge of himself and his position in society and the world, then he has little chance to relate to anything else.

6. We want all black men to be exempt from military service.

    We believe that Black people should not be forced to fight in the military service to defend a racist government that does not protect us. We will not fight and kill other people of color in the world who, like black people, are being victimized by the white racist government of America. We will protect ourselves from the force and violence of the racist police and the racist military, by whatever means necessary.

7. We want an immediate end to POLICE BRUTALITY and MURDER of black people.

    We believe we can end police brutality in our black community by organizing black self-defense groups that are dedicated to defending our black community from racist police oppression and brutality. The Second Amendment to the Constitution of the United States gives a right to bear arms. We therefore believe that all black people should themselves for self-defense.

8. We want freedom for all black men held in federal, state, county and city prisons and jails.

    We believe that all black people should be released from the many jails and prisons because they have not received a fair and impartial trial.

9. We want all black people when brought to trial to be tried in court by a jury of their peer group or people from their black communities, as defined by the Constitution of the United States.

    We believe that the courts should follow the United States Constitution so that black people will receive fair trials. The 14th Amendment of the U.S. Constitution gives a man a right to be tried by his peer group. A peer is a person from a similar economic, social, religious, geographical, environmental, historical and racial background. To do this the court will be forced to select a jury from the black community from which the black defendant came. We have been, and are being tried by all-white juries that have no understanding of the "average reasoning man" of the Black community.

10. We want land, bread, housing, education, clothing, justice and peace. And as our major political objective, a United Nations-supervised plebiscite to be held throughout the black colony in which only black colonial subjects will be allowed to participate, for the purpose of determining the will of black people as to their national destiny.

    When, in the course of human events, it becomes necessary for one people to dissolve the political bands which have connected them with another, and to assume, among the powers of the earth, the separate and equal station to which the laws of nature and nature's God entitle them, a decent respect to the opinions of mankind requires that they should declare the causes which impel them to the separation.

    We hold these truths to be self-evident, that all men are created equal; that they are endowed by their Creator with certain unalienable rights; that among these are life, liberty, and the pursuit of happiness. That, to secure these rights, governments are instituted among men, deriving their just powers from the consent of the governed; that, whenever any form of government becomes destructive to these ends, it is the right of the people to alter or abolish it, and to institute a new government, laying its foundation on such principles, and organizing its powers in such form, as to them shall seem most likely to effect their safety and happiness. Prudence, indeed, will dictate that governments long established should not be changed for light and transient causes; and, accordingly, all experience has shown, that mankind are more disposed to suffer, while evils are sufferable, than to right themselves by abolishing the forms which they are accustomed. *But, when a long train of abuses and usurpations pursuing invariably the same object, evinces a design to reduce them under absolute despotism, it is their right, it is their duty, to throw off such government, and to provide new guards for their future security.*

(Reprinted from *The Black Panther*, Sept 14, 1968, page 7.)

Rules of the Black Panther Party

Every member of the BLACK PANTHER PARTY throughout this country of racist America must abide by these rules as functional members of this party. CENTRAL COMMITTEE members, CENTRAL STAFFS, and LOCAL STAFFS, including all captains subordinate to either national, state, and local leadership of the BLACK PANTHER PARTY will enforce these rules. Length of suspension or other disciplinary action necessary for violation of these rules will depend on national decisions by national, state or state area, and local committees and staffs where said rule or rules of the BLACK PANTHER PARTY WERE VIOLATED.

Every member of the party must know these verbatim by heart. And apply them daily. Each member must report any violation of these rules to their leadership or they are counter-revolutionary and are also subjected to suspension by the BLACK PANTHER PARTY.

THE RULES ARE:

1. No party member can have narcotics or weed in his possession while doing party work.

2. Any party found shooting narcotics will be expelled from the party.

3. No party member can be DRUNK while doing daily party work.

4. No party member will violate rules relating to office work, general meetings of the BLACK PANTHER PARTY, and meetings of the BLACK PANTHER PARTY ANYWHERE.

5. No party member will USE, POINT, or FIRE a weapon of any kind unnecessarily or accidentally at anyone.

6. No party member can join any other army force other than the BLACK LIBERATION ARMY.

7. No party member can have a weapon in his possession while DRUNK or loaded off narcotics or weed.

8. No party member will commit any crimes against other party members or BLACK people at all, and cannot steal or take from the people, not even a needle or a piece of thread.

9. When arrested BLACK PANTHER MEMBERS will give only name, address, and will sign nothing. Legal first aid must be understood by all Party members.

10. The Ten Point Program and platform of the BLACK PANTHER PARTY must be known and understood by each Party member.

11. Party Communications must be National and Local.

12. The 10–10–10 program should be known by all members and also understood by all members.

13. All Finance officers will operate under the jurisdiction of the Ministry of Finance.

14. Each person will submit a report of daily work.

15. Each Sub-Section Leader, Section Leader, Lieutenant, and Captain must submit Daily reports of work.

16. All Panthers must learn to operate and service weapons correctly.

17. All Leadership personnel who expel a member must submit this information to the Editor of the Newspaper, so that it will be published in the paper and will be known by all chapters and branches.

18. Political Education Classes are mandatory for general membership.

19. Only office personnel assigned to respective offices each day should be there. All others are to sell papers and do Political work out in the community including Captains, Section Leaders, etc.

20. COMMUNICATIONS- all chapters must submit weekly reports in writing to the National Headquarters.

21. All Branches must implement First Aid and/or Medical Cadres.

22. All Chapters, Branches, and components of the BLACK PANTHER PARTY must submit a monthly Financial Report to the Ministry of Finance, and also the Central Committee.

23. Everyone in a leadership position must read no less than two hours per day to keep abreast of the changing political situation.

24. No chapter or branch shall accept grants, poverty funds, money or any other aid from any government agency without contacting the National Headquarters.

25. All chapters must adhere to the policy and the ideology laid down by the CENTRAL COMMITTEE of the BLACK PANTHER PARTY.

26. All Branches must submit weekly reports in writing to their respective Chapters.

(Reprinted from *The Black Panther*, Sept 28, 1970, page 18.)

Appendix C
Membership of the Milwaukee Branch

1969 MILWAUKEE PANTHERS

Name	Rank	Sources
Nate Bellamy	Lieutenant of Information	*Milwaukee Journal* Oct. 13, 1969, p. 9
Walter Chesser	Deputy Minister of Defense	*Milwaukee Sentinel* Feb. 1, 1969, p. 13.
Booker Collins	NA	*Milwaukee Courier* Sept. 27, 1969, p. 1
Allen Crawford	NA	*Milwaukee Journal* June 18, 1969, p. 1.
Paul Crayton	Lieutenant of Religion	*Milwaukee Journal* June 18, 1969, p. 1
Lynn Epps	NA	*Milwaukee Courier* June 14, 1969, p. 1
Dakin Gentry	Deputy Field Marshall	*Milwaukee Sentinel* May 23, 1969, p. 20
Howard Haralson	Lieutenant of Education	*Milwaukee Journal* Oct. 13, 1969, part 2, p. 2
Donald Jackson	Lieutenant of Finance	*Milwaukee Sentinel* July 30, 1969, p. 8
Ronald Jefferies	NA	*Milwaukee Sentinel* July 18, 1970, p. 1

1969 MILWAUKEE PANTHERS Continued

Name	Rank	Sources
Earl Levrettes	NA	*Milwaukee Courier* Sept. 27, 1969, p. 1
Leslie Mays	NA	*Milwaukee Sentinel* June 19, 1969, p. 1
George Owens	NA	*Milwaukee Sentinel* Oct. 23, 1969, p. 14
Abdullah Salahadyn	Deputy Minister of Religion	*Milwaukee Journal* Mar. 23, 1969, part 2, p. 8
Jackie Simpson	NA	*Kaleidoscope* June 20-July 3, 1969, p. 3
Ronald Starks	Deputy Minister of Labor	*Milwaukee Journal* Mar. 23, 1969, part 2, p. 8
John Trenton	Field Lieutenant	*Milwaukee Sentinel* June 9, 1969, part 2, p. 11
Felix Welch	Field Lieutenant	*Milwaukee Sentinel* Sept. 27, 1969, p. 1
Jessie White	Security Sergeant	*Milwaukee Courier* June 14, 1969, p. 1

1973 Milwaukee Panthers

Name	Rank	Source
Doris Brown	NA	Michael McGee.
Lyndell Fields	NA	*Milwaukee Courier* Mar. 30, 1974, p. 18
Roy Maxie	Administrator of Breakfast Program	*UWM Post Magazine* Nov. 1973, p. 1

1973 Milwaukee Panthers continued

Name	Rank	Source
Geneva McGee	Director of the People's Free Health Center	*Milwaukee Courier* Mar. 30, 1974, p. 18
Michael McGee	Coordinator	Michael McGee.
Penelope McGee	NA	*Milwaukee Courier* Mar 30, 1974, p. 18
Charlotte Nash	Assistant Director of People's Free Health Center	Milwaukee Courier Mar 29, 1975, p. 14
Ronald Starks	Co-Chairman	*Milwaukee Courier* May 11, 1974, p. 3
Kenneth Williamson	Minister of Information	Black Panther Party Clippings File.

(These are not complete lists of the membership of the Milwaukee branch, but only those names found in various public records.)

Appendix D

A Proposal of the Milwaukee Branch for Community Control of the Milwaukee Police Department

I.   Community control means a citizen elected structure to deal with both the particular problems of each of our communities and the general problems we face together in the city of Milwaukee.

A.   Structure

1.   Community control of police means citizen boards in each police district chosen in low budget, non-partisan elections.

a.   District board members will live in the area, be 18 years or older, hold no other public office, nor serve at the same time on the Milwaukee police force.

b.   Special nonpartisan elections will be low budget with a small amount of city funds provided for each candidate for their campaigning to insure that wealth is not a criteria for getting elected.

c.   The district boards will oversee police affairs in their area.

2.   Community control of police means two community elected representatives from each local district to serve on a Citywide Police Commission.

a.   The Citywide Police Commission will have two representatives from each district. One will be the president of each local board and the other a citizen elected at large from each district.

b. The Citywide Police Commission will coordinate city-wide functions.

3. Community control of police means that the public will have access to records of meetings and finances and will participate fully.

a. All meetings will be public. Special measures (like the times and place, full right to speak at meetings, etc.) will insure full citizen participation. Citizens may circulate petitions to call special meetings when they deem necessary.

b. All records of meetings and financial reports be readily available to the public on a regular monthly basis.

c. The right of all citizens to privacy shall be well guarded.

II. Community control of police means that citizen elected bodies will be responsive and responsible to the communities.

A. Functions- The powers and duties of the District Board: 'Each District Board shall set policy, procedures, and regulations with respect to all affairs of the police in its district that will insure the safety, justice, and general well being of the citizenry of the city of Milwaukee.'

1. Community control of police means that local district boards have fiscal powers.

a. Each board will submit a yearly budget to the Citywide Commission for their district.

2. Community control of police means that local district boards have personnel (hiring, firing, transferring) powers.

a. Each district board will select a district commander who has at least 5 years experience and resides in the district.

b. Each district board will review the personnel selected by the district commander with the power to disapprove.

3. Community control of police means that police live in the district where they work so that they may be more sensitive to the needs of their community.

4. Community control of police means that local district boards will hold public hearings on and be able to act on grievances.

a. Each board will hear citizen grievances against the police and act on them according to guidelines established by the Citywide Commission.

b. Each district board will likewise hear suggestions and complaints about the administration of police affairs from police department employees.

B. The Powers and duties of the Citywide Commission: 'The Citywide Police Commissions establishes uniform citywide regulations which do not interfere with local boards and resolves any possible conflicts between districts.'

1. Community control of police means that the Citywide Commissions has fiscal power.

a. They will submit a yearly budget to the city council and allocate money as needed to the district boards and to citywide departments.

2. Community control of police means that the Citywide Commission has personnel powers.

a. The Citywide Commission will appoint a coordinator of police with considerable experience to oversee interdistrict functions and coordinate citywide agencies like traffic and training.

b. The Citywide Commission shall set guidelines for hiring, firing, disciplining, transferring and promotion policies without interfering with powers of the local boards.

3. Community control of policy means that the Citywide Commission will coordinate necessary functions and set general policy guidelines and procedures.

    a. The Citywide Commission will set uniform grievance procedures and hear unresolved disputes from local boards.

    b. The Citywide Commission will set policies for training and recruiting police.

    c. The Citywide Commission will coordinate communication between local boards.

4. Community control of police means that the Citywide Commission will hear any charges of conflict of interest or failure to make full disclosure of finances against any local or Citywide Commission member.

(Reprinted from *The Black Panther*, August 3, 1974.)

A Sampling of Locations of Black Panther Party Community Programs Nationwide

BREAKFAST PROGRAMS

Branch	Location	# served (estimated)	Date established
Albany, NY	NA	NA	By Dec. 27, 1969
Baltimore	1209 N. Eden St.	150 daily	By Dec. 27, 1969
Berkeley	3106 Shuttuck Ave.	NA	By Dec. 27, 1969
Boston	375 Bluehill Ave.	NA	By Dec. 27, 1969
Brooklyn	180 Sutter Ave.	NA	By Dec. 27, 1969
Chicago	1512 S. Pulaski St.	200 daily	By Apr. 27, 1969
Chicago	500 E. 37th St.	300 daily	By Apr. 27, 1969
Chicago	2350 W. Madison	NA	By Dec. 27, 1969
Cleveland	NA	NA	By Apr. 17, 1971
Denver	2834 W. Lafayette	NA	By Dec. 27, 1969
Des Moines	Forest Ave. Baptist Church	75 daily	By Apr. 27, 1969
Eugene, OR	1671 ½ Pearl	NA	By Dec. 27, 1969

BREAKFAST PROGRAMS continued

Branch	Location	# served (estimated)	Date established
Harlem	Friendship Baptist Church	NA	By May 19, 1969
Indianapolis	113 W. 30th St.	NA	By July 19, 1969
Jersey City	384 Pacific Ave.	NA	By Dec. 27, 1969
Kansas City	St. Stephen Baptist Church		By May 11, 1969
Kansas City	Paseo Baptist Church	450 daily/combined	By May 11, 1969
Los Angeles	4115 S. Central Ave.	NA	By Dec. 27, 1969
Los Angeles	Watts Community	NA	By Dec. 27, 1969
Los Angeles	Watts Headquarters	NA	By Dec. 27, 1969
Milwaukee	2121 N. 1st Street	150 daily	By July 5, 1969
New Haven	35 Syldan	NA	By Dec. 27, 1969
New York	2026 7th Ave.	NA	By Dec. 27, 1969
Oakland	St. Augustine Episcopal Church	165 daily	By Apr. 27, 1969
Queens, NY	108–60 NY Blvd.	NA	By Dec. 27, 1969
Peekskill, NY	22 Nelson Ave.	50 daily	By July 5, 1969
Philadelphia	1928 Columbia	NA	By Dec. 27, 1969
Richmond, CA	520 Bissell St.	NA	By Dec. 27, 1969
Sacramento	Oak Park Unity Church	NA	By Sept. 22, 1969

BREAKFAST PROGRAMS continued

Branch	Location	# served (estimated)	Date established
San Francisco	Sacred Heart Parish	95 daily	By Apr. 27, 1969
San Francisco	922 Gilmore	80 daily	By Apr. 27, 1969
San Francisco	181 Hilltop Rd.	85 daily	By Apr. 27, 1969
Seattle	1127 ½ 34th St.	NA	By Dec. 27, 1969
Staten Island	232 Jersey St.	NA	By Dec. 27, 1969
Vallejo, CA	Party Headquarters	110 daily	By Apr. 27, 1969
White Plains, NY	159 S. Lexington	NA	By Dec. 27, 1969

LIBERATION SCHOOLS

Berkeley	Good Sheppard Church	25 daily	By July 12, 1969
Bronx	NA	NA	By Feb. 20, 1971
Los Angeles	5022 S. Central Ave.	NA	By Apr. 9, 1977
Oakland	NA	NA	By Mar. 31, 1973
Queens	Malcolm X Center	90 daily	By Aug. 16, 1969
San Francisco	Ridgeport Methodist Church	25 daily	By Aug. 2, 1969
Seattle	NA	NA	By Sept. 13, 1969
Staten Island	NA	20 daily	By Aug. 30, 1969

LIBERATION SCHOOLS continued

Branch	Location	# served (estimated)	Date established
Winston-Salem, NC	NA	40 daily	By July 4, 1970

HEALTH CLINICS

Branch	Location	# served	Date established
Berkeley	3236 Adeline Ave.	NA	By May 15, 1971
Boston and Ruggles	Corner of Tremont	NA	By June 13, 1970
Chicago	NA	NA	By Mar. 28, 1970
Cleveland	NA	NA	By Sept. 11, 1971
Kansas City	NA	NA	By Aug. 16, 1969
Milwaukee	2636 N. 3rd St.	NA	By May 18, 1974
New Haven	27 Dixwell Ave.	NA	By Jan. 30, 1971
Palo Alto, CA	2369 University Ave.	NA	By Sept. 23, 1972
Seattle	NA	NA	By Dec. 6, 1969
Staten Island	NA	NA	By Aug. 30, 1969
Washington, D.C.	4025 9th St.	NA	By June 9, 1973

All information is from *The Black Panther*. The dates consulted are those listed under date established.

This is not a complete listing of every Panther community program, or of all locations of breakfast programs, liberation schools, or medical clinics.

NA= **Not available.**

Notes

NOTES TO THE INTRODUCTION

1. Michael McGee, interview on WNOV with author, Milwaukee, Wisconsin; Apr 15, 2003, tape in possession of author.
2. Arwin D Smallwood, *The Atlas of African-American History and Politics: From the Slave Trade to Modern Times* (Boston: McGraw-Hill, 1998), 152.
3. *Power!*, vol. 9, Eyes on the Prize, prod. and dir. Louis J. Massiah & Terry K. Rockefeller, 60 min., 1990, videocassette, 33:00.
4. Cleveland Sellers with Robert Terrell, *The River of No Return: The Autobiography of a Black Militant and the Life and Death of SNCC* (William Morrow & Company, 1973; reprint, Jackson: University Press of Mississippi, 1990), 263, (page citations are to the reprint edition).
5. *Milwaukee Star*, 30 Oct 1971, 1; *University of Wisconsin-Milwaukee (UWM) Post*, 1 May 1970, 5; *Milwaukee Star*, 3 Apr 1971, 1; *UWM Post*, 26 Sept 1969, *Milwaukee Sentinel*, 7 March 1970, 5; *Milwaukee Sentinel*, 16 Sept 1970; *Milwaukee Sentinel*, 15 Sept 1970, 11.
6. *Milwaukee Star*, 30 Oct 1971, 1; *University of Wisconsin-Milwaukee Post*, 1 May 1970, 5; *Milwaukee Star*, 3 Apr 1971, 1; *UWM Post*, 26 Sept 1969, 7; *UWM Post*, 17 Oct 1969, 3; *UWM Post*, 9 Dec 1969, 12; *UWM Post*, 10 Sept 1974, 5; *Milwaukee Sentinel*, 7 March 1970, 5; *Milwaukee Sentinel*, 16 Sept 1970, 8; *Milwaukee Sentinel*, 15 Sept 1970, 11; Black Panther Party, Social Action Vertical File, MSS-577, box 6, Wisconsin State Historical Society, Madison.
7. John Patrick Diggins, *The Rise and Fall of the American Left* (New York: W. W. Norton & Company: 1992), 260.
8. Former FBI agent Curtis R. Jimerson, phone interview by author, 23 Nov 1997, transcript in possession of author.
9. David Hilliard and Lewis Cole, *This Side of Glory: The Autobiography of David Hilliard and the Story of the Black Panther Party* (Boston: Little, Brown and Company, 1993), vi.

10. Don A. Schanche, *The Panther Paradox: A Liberal's Dilemma* (New York: David McKay, Co., 1971), xi,

11. Ibid., 231.

12. Norman Hill, ed., *The Black Panther Menace: America's Neo-Nazis* (New York: Popular Library, 1971), 55, 60.

13. Errol Anthony Henderson's "Shadow of a Clue" in *Liberation, Imagination and the Black Panther Party*, eds., Kathleen Cleaver and George Katsiaficas (Routledge: New York, 2001), 206.

14. *Higher Learning*, prod. and dir. John Singleton, 127 min., Columbia Pictures, 1995, videocassette, 1:20.

15. *The Sixties*, part 2, prod. and dir. Jim Chorry, 90 min, National Broadcasting Company, 1999, videocassette, 3:15.

16. John A. Wood, *The Panthers and the Militias: Brothers Under the Skin?* (Lanham, NY: University Press of America, Inc., 2002), ix.

17. Contrary to what scholars like Wood claim, self-defense is not synonymous with violence. The use of violence implies the use of aggression, but practitioners of self-defense are obviously not aggressors, because they are defending themselves from attack. Those who embraced non-violent civil disobedience as a form of protest, however, did not have the option to defend themselves. Advocates of non-violence believed they would be perceived as unruly protestors, and that they would loose sympathy for their cause, if they fought back.

18. Wood, 11.

19. JoNina M. Abron's article, entitled, "'Serving the People'": The Survival Programs of the Black Panther Party" does examine the community programs of the Party, but it only provides an overview of the Panther's community programs on the national level.

20. Charles Jones, ed. *The Black Panther Party: Reconsidered* (Baltimore: Black Classic Press, 1998), 1.

21. Huey Newton, *Revolutionary Suicide* (Harcourt Brace Javonovich, Inc., 1973; reprint, Writers and Readers Publishing, Inc., 1995), 166, (page citations are to the reprint edition).

22. Jonathan Coleman, *Long Way to Go: Black and White in America* (New York: Atlantic Monthly Press, 1997), 284.

23. Stokely Carmichael and Charles V. Hamilton, *Black Power: The Politics of Liberation in America* (New York: Random House, 1967), 84.

24. Quoted in Paula Pfeffer, *A. Philip Randolph: Pioneer of the Civil Rights Movement* (Baton Rouge: Louisiana State University Press, 1990), 57.

25. Newton, *Revolutionary Suicide*, 167.

26. William Van Deburg, *New Day in Babylon: The Black Power Movement and American Culture, 1965-1975* (Chicago: University of Chicago Press, 1992), 23.

27. Ibid., 48.

28. David Chalmers, *And the Crooked Places Made Straight: The Struggle for Social Change in the 1960s*, 2nd ed. (Baltimore: The Johns Hopkins University Press, 1996), 70; *Berkeley in the Sixties*, New York, First Run Features,

prod. and dir. By Mark Kitchell, written by Stephen Most, Mark Kitchell and Susan Griffin, 117 min, 1990, videocassette.

29. Herbert Aptheker, ed. *A Documentary History of the Negro People in the United States*, vol. 7, *From the Alabama Protests to the Death of Martin Luther King, Jr.*, with a foreword by Angela Y. Davis (New York: Citadel Press, 1994), 375.

30. Coleman, 6.

31. *UWM Post*, 20 May 1969, 9.

32. Elaine Brown, *A Taste of Power: A Black Women's Story* (New York: Pantheon Books, 1992) 142; Bobby Seale, *Seize the Time* (Random House, 1970, reprint; Baltimore: Black Classic Free Press, 1991), 219.

33. Charles E. Jones and Judson L. Jeffries "'Don't Believe the Hype': Debunking the Panther Mythology" in *The Black Panther Party Reconsidered*, 38.

34. Tracye Matthews, "'No One Ever Asks, What a Man's Role in the Revolution is': Gender and the Politics of the Black Panther Party, 1966-1971" in *The Black Panther Party: Reconsidered*, 271.

35. Maulana Karenga, *The Quotable Karenga*, Wisconsin State Historical Society Pamphlet Collection, n.d., 37.

36. Angela Davis, *Angela Davis: An Autobiography* (New York: Random House, 1974), 158.

37. Brown, 368.

38. Angela D. LeBlanc Ernest, "The Most Qualified Person to Handle the Job: Black Panther Party Women, 1966-1982," in *The Black Panther Party: Reconsidered*, 322.

39. Brown, 391; *Black Panther* (Oakland), 31 May 1969, 5; "Black Panther Sisters Speak About Women's Liberation," Wisconsin State Historical Society Pamphlet Collection, n.d.

40. *Black Panther*, 19 July 1969, 9; *Black Panther*, 21 June 1969, 18; Matthews, in *The Black Panther Party: Reconsidered*, 289.

41. *Black Panther*, 31 May 1969, 5; Jones, 13; Matthews, in *The Black Panther Party: Reconsidered* 270; *Black Panther*, 20 Apr 1974, 5; LeBlanc-Ernest, in *The Black Panther Party: Reconsidered*, 311.

42. *Black Panther*, 7 Dec 1968, 16; *Black Panther*, 21 Nov 1970; 15; *Black Panther*, 13 Apr 1974; *Black Panther* 27 Oct 1973, 17; *Black Panther* 24 Nov 1973, 14; *Black Panther*, 16 Feb 1974; 9; *Black Panther*, 7 Sept 1974, 10; *Black Panther*, 6 Apr 1974, 17; *Black Panther*, 9 Mar 1974, 4; *Black Panther*, 5 Oct 1974, 1; *Black Panther*, 16 Mar 1974; 1; *Black Panther*, 17 Aug 1974, 9; *Black Panther*, 22 Dec 1973, 5; *Black Panther* 18 May 1974; 9; *Black Panther*, 4 May 1974; 5; *Black Panther*, 27 Oct 1973, 7; *Black Panther*, 2 Mar 1974, 5; *Black Panther*, 9 Feb 1974, 17.

43. Brown, 115.

44. Brown, 9, 192; "Black Panther Sisters Talk About Women's Liberation."; Regina Jennings, "Why I Joined the Party: An Africana Womanist Reflection," in *The Black Panther Party: Reconsidered*, 257; LeBlanc-Ernest, in *The Black Panther Party: Reconsidered*, 311.

45. McGee.

46. Matthews, in *The Black Panther Party: Reconsidered*, 293.
47. *Black Panther*, 6 Apr 1974. 17; *Black Panther*, 27 Oct 1973, 7.
48. Former Black Panther Michael Fultz, interview by author, 16 Nov 1998, transcript in possession of author.
49. Van Deburg, 23.

NOTES TO CHAPTER ONE

1. Gerda Lerner, ed. *Black Women in White America: A Documentary History* (Pantheon Books: 1972; reprint, New York, Vintage Books, 1973), 64 (page citations are to the reprint edition).
2. James M. McPherson, *The Negro's Civil War: How American Blacks Felt and Acted During the War for the Union* (New York: Ballantine Books, 1965; reprint, Pantheon Books, 1982), 71–73 (page citations are to the reprint addition).
3. Robert Cruden, *The Negro in Reconstruction* (Englewood Cliffs, New Jersey: Prentice Hall, 1969), 151–152.
4. Herbert Shapiro, *White Violence and Black Response: From Reconstruction to Montgomery* (Amherst: University of Massachusetts Press, 1988), 11.
5. Shapiro, 13.
6. Smallwood, 106–107.
7. Paula Giddings, *When and Where I Enter: The Impact of Black Women on Race and Sex in America* (New York: W. Morrow, 1984; reprint, New York: Bantam Books, 1988), 17 (page citations are to the reprint edition).
8. Ibid., 20.
9. Shapiro, 100.
10. W.E.B. DuBois, quoted in Nathan Hare's foreword in *The Souls of Black Folk* (1903; reprint, New York: Signet Classic, 1982), xx, (page citations are to the reprint edition).
11. Ibid.
12. Lee E. Williams and Lee E. Williams II, *Anatomy of Four Race Riots: Racial Conflict in Knoxville, Elaine (Arkansas), Tulsa and Chicago, 1919–1921*, with a foreword by Roy Wilkins (Oxford: University and College Press of Mississippi, 1972), 38–39, 44, 47, 53.
13. Michael D' Orso, *Like Judgment Day: The Ruin and Redemption of a Town Called Rosewood* (New York: G.P. Putnam's Sons, 1996), 1–13.
14. Shapiro, 186.
15. Robin D.G. Kelly, *Hammer and Hoe: Alabama Communists During the Great Depression* (Chapel Hill: University of North Carolina Press, 1990), 41.
16. Ibid., 45.
17. Herbert Aptheker, ed. *A Documentary History of Negro People in the United States, vol. 4, From the New Deal to the End of World War II,*

(New York: Citadel Press, 1974; reprint, New York: Citadel Press, 1992), 193 (page citations are to the reprint addition); Jim Meriweather, a member of the Sharecropper's Union, was lynched by whites on August 22, 1935, near Sandy Ridge, Alabama.

18. Theodore Rosengarten, *All God's Dangers: The Life of Nate Shaw* (New York: Avon Books, 1974), xiii 104, 105, 171, 179, 322, 323, 327–329, 539, 571, 582.

19. John Egerton, *Speak Now Against the Day: The Generation Before the Civil Rights Movement in the South* (Chapel Hill: University of North Carolina Press, 1994), 363–364.

20. Tim Tyson, *Radio Free Dixie: Robert F. Williams and the Roots of the Black Power Movement* (Chapel Hill: University of North Carolina Press, 1999), 54.

21. Tyson, *Radio Free Dixie*, 215.

22. Ibid., 215.

23. John Dittmer, *Local People: The Struggle for Civil Rights in Mississippi* (Urbana: University of Illinois Press, 1994; reprint, Urbana: University of Illinois Press, 1995), 31–32.

24. Ibid., 106.

25. Ibid., 47.

26. Ibid, 47.

27. Ibid., 49.

28. Taylor Branch, *Parting the Waters: America in the King Years, 1954–1963* (New York: Touchstone Books, 1989), 162, 165, 179.

29. Robert Carl Cohen, *Black Crusader: A Biography of Robert Franklin Williams* (Secaucus, New Jersey: Lyle Stuart, Inc. 1972), 85; Robert F. Williams, *Negroes With Guns*, with a foreword by Gloria House and an introduction by Tim Tyson (New York: Marzani & Munsell, Inc., 1962; reprint, Detroit: Wayne State University Press, 1998), xvii, xix (page citations are to the reprint edition).

30. Richard Dalfiume, "The 'Forgotten Years' of the Negro Revolution," *Journal of American History* 60, no. 1 (1968–1969): 97; Harvard Sitkoff, "Racial Militancy and Interracial Violence in the Second World War," *Journal of American History* 58, no. 3 (1971): 661; Williams and Williams, 9.

31. Williams, xix, 14.

32. Cohen, 352–353, 361.

33. Williams, 24–26.

34. Ibid., 76.

35. Elliot Rudwick and August Meier, *From Plantation to Ghetto*, 3rd ed. (New York: Hill and Wang, 1976; reprint, New York: Hill and Wang, 1996), 303 (Page citations are to the reprint edition).

36. Gloria House in *Negroes With Guns*, xi.

37. Williams, 4.

38. Ibid., 6.

39. Ibid., 4, 6.

40. Ibid., 83.

41. Tim Tyson, "Robert F. Williams, 'Black Power,' and the Roots of the African American Freedom Struggle," *Journal of American History* 85, no. 2 (1998): 544, 570.

42. Tyson, *Radio Free Dixie*, 3.

43. Roy Wilkins with Tom Mathews, *Standing Fast: The Autobiography of Roy Wilkins* (Viking Press, 1982; reprint, New York: Penguin Books, 1984), 265 (page citations are to the reprint edition).

44. Branch, *Parting the Waters*, 460.

45. Clayborne Carson, *In Struggle: SNCC and the Black Awakening of the 1960's* (Cambridge, MA: Harvard University Press, 1981), 299.

46. Branch, *Parting the Waters*, 781.

47. Howell Raines, *My Soul is Rested: Movement Days in the Deep South Remembered* (Ontario, Canada: Longham Canada Limited, 1977; reprint, New York: Penguin Books, Inc., 1987), 114–115, 265, 267 (page citations are to the reprint edition); The Youth of the Rural Organizing and Cultural Center, *Minds Stayed on Freedom: The Civil Rights Struggle in the Rural South*, with an introduction by Jay MacLeod (Boulder, Co.: Westview Press, 1991), 13, 24–25.

48. Carson, 122.

49. Dittmer, 188–189.

50. Ibid., 267–268.

51. Ibid., 278.

52. Tyson, *Radio Free Dixie*, 153, 165.

53. Dittmer, 249.

54. Carson, 164.

55. Taylor Branch, *Pillar of Fire: America in the King Years, 1963–1965* (New York: Simon & Schuster, 1998), 66.

56. Ibid., 111.

57. Ibid., 162.

58. Branch, *Pillar of Fire*, 257; Malcolm X, *The Autobiography of Malcolm X as told to Alex Haley*, with an introduction by M.S. Handler (New York: Ballantine Books, 1964), 415.

59. Branch, *Pillar of Fire*, 381.

60. Lance Hill, *The Deacons for Defense: Armed Resistance and the Civil Rights Movement* (Chapel Hill: University of North Carolina Press, 2004), 2, 4; Raines, 416, 418, 420, 421; Federal Bureau of Investigation (FBI), Special Agent in Charge (SAC), New Orleans, to Director, January 6, 1964, HQ 157–2466.

61. Aptheker, vol. 7, 374.

62. Sellers, 166.

63. Hill, 8.

64. FBI, SAC, New Orleans, to Director, January 6, 1964, HQ 157–2466.

65. Hill, 2.

66. Ibid., 5.

67. Meier & Rudwick, 304–305.

68. Judith Stein, *The World of Marcus Garvey: Race and Class in Modern Society* (Baton Rouge, LA: Louisiana State University Press, 1986; reprint, 1991), 30.

69. Amy Jacques-Garvey, ed., *Philosophies and Opinions of Marcus Garvey*, with a preface by Hollis R. Lynch (New York: Antheneum, 1923; reprint, New York: Antheneum, 1977), 137 (page citations are to the reprint edition); Rupert Lewis & Patrick Bryan, eds., *Garvey: His Work and Impact* (Trenton, NJ: Africa World Press, 1991), 68, 78; Theodore G. Vincent, *Black Power and the Garvey Movement* (Berkeley: Ramparts Press, n.d.), 102.

70. Lenwood G. Davis, ed. *Daddy Grace: An Annotated Bibliography* (New York: Greenwood Press, 1992), x, 5–6.

71. Herbert Aptheker, vol. 4, 157

72. Ibid., 159.

73. Robert Weisbrot, *Father Divine and the Struggle for Racial Equality* (Urbana: University of Illinois Press, 1983), 35.

74. Sara Harris, *Father Divine*, with an introduction by John Henrik Clarke (Double Day & Co., 1953; reprint, New York: Collier Books, 1971), 50–51.

75. Ibid., 52, 53, 227.

76. Jill Watts, *God, Harlem U.S.A: The Father Divine Story* (Berkeley: University of California Press, 1992; reprint, 1995), 61, (page citations are to the reprint edition). .

77. *I Remember Harlem: The Depression Years, 1930–1940*, prod. and dir. William Miles, 58 min., Films for the Humanities and Sciences, 1991, videocassette, 33:00–38:00; Vincent, 225; Watts, 75.

78. Malcolm X, 298–302

79. Hugh Pearson, *The Shadow of the Panther: Huey Newton and the Price of Black Power in America* (Reading, MA.: Addison-Wesley, 1994), 347.

NOTES TO CHAPTER TWO

1. Martin Luther King, Jr., *Why We Can't Wait* (1964; reprint, Penguin Books, n.d.), 37.

2. George Jackson, *Soledad Brother* (New York: Coward-McCann, 1970; reprint, Chicago: Lawrence Hill Books, 1994), 168 (page citations are to the reprint edition).

3. *A Place of Rage*, prod. and dir. Pratibha Parmar, 52 min., Women Make Movies, 1991, videocassette, 2:15.

4. Frantz Fanon, *The Wretched of the Earth* (New York: Grove Press, Inc., 1961; reprint, 1968), 60 (page citations are to the reprint edition).

5. *A Nation of Law?*, vol. 12, Eyes on the Prize, prod. and dir. Terry K. Rock-efellar, Thomas Orr & Louis J. Massiah, 60 min., 1990, videocassette, 6:00.

6. *UWM Post*, 9 Apr 1968, 5.

7. Roy E. Finkenbine, *Sources of the African-American Past: Primary Sources in American History* (New York: Longman Publishers, 1997), 185.

8. Jones and Jeffries, in *The Black Panther Party: Reconsidered*, 25.

9. Peter M. Bergman, *The Chronological History of the Negro in America* (New York: Mentor Books, 1969), 595.

10. Van Deburg, 19–28.

11. Newton, *Revolutionary Suicide*, 5, 116.

12. *Report of the National Advisory Commission on Civil Disorders* (New York: E.P. Dutton & Company, Inc., 1968), 1.

13. *Power!*, 36:35–36:44; *Black Panther*, 20 June 1970, 22; Hilliard & Cole, 3; *Los Angeles Times*, 31 Jan 1972, part 1, 19; Van Deburg, 155.

14. Newton, *Revolutionary Suicide*, 330.

15. Paul Chevigny, *Cops and Rebels: A Study of Provocation* (New York: Pantheon Books, 1972), 87; Newton, *Revolutionary Suicide*, 330; *Milwaukee Sentinel*, 14 May 1971, 1; Van Deburg, 159.

16. Van Deburg, 159.

17. Jimerson.

18. DeLoach, Cartha. *Hoover's FBI: The Inside Story by Hoover's Trusted Liaison.* (Washington D.C.: Regnery Publish, Inc., 1995), 290; *Power!*, 27:00; Chevigny, 99, 145, 365.

19. *A Nation of Law?*, 7:15, 12:45

20. Winston Grady-Willis, "The Black Panther Party: State Repression and Political Prisoners," in *The Black Panther Party: Reconsidered*, 365–366.

21. Ward Churchill and Jim Vander Wall, *Agents of Repression: The FBI's Secret Wars Against the Black Panther Party and the American Indian Movement* (Boston: South End Press, 1990; reprint, 1998), 47–48 (page citations are to the reprint edition).

22. Churchill and Vander Wall, 53.

23. *Black Panther*, 2 Feb 1969, 6.

24. Citizen Research and Investigation Committee and Louis E. Tackwood, 105–106; Churchill and Vander Wall, 42; *Milwaukee Courier*, 20 Sept 1969, 1; Huey Newton, "War Against the Panthers: A Study of Repression in America" (Ph.D. diss., University of California, Santa-Cruz, 1980), 103.

25. *Black Panther*, 13 Dec 1975, 3, 4; *A Nation of Law?*, 12:45; Churchill and Vander Wall, 44, 49, 65.

26. *Los Angeles Times*, 4 Apr 1972, part 1, 8; *Los Angeles Times*, 17 Mar 1972, part 1, 24; Citizens Research and Investigation Committee & Tackwood, 25, 30; Kenneth O'Reilly, *Black Americans: The FBI Files* (New York: Carroll & Graf Publishers, 1994), 49–50; Steve Weissman, ed., *Big Brother and the Holding Company* (Palo Alto, CA: Ramparts Press, 1974), 318; *UWM Post*, 25 Sept 1970, 2; *Greater Milwaukee Star*, 20 Dec 1969,

3; Henry Maier, box 9, folder 25, University of Wisconsin-Milwaukee Manuscript Collections, University of Wisconsin-Milwaukee Archives.

27. Jones, 1.

28. Citizens Research and Investigation Committee & Tackwood, 96.

29. *Milwaukee Courier*, 17 May 1969, 8; *Milwaukee Courier*, 12 July 1969, 10; *Milwaukee Courier*, 9 Aug 1969, 2.

30. Newton, "War Against the Panthers," 9.

31. Van Deburg, 3; Richard T. Shaefer, *Racial and Ethnic Groups*, 4th ed. (Harper Collins Publishers, 1990), 231; *UWM Post*, 10 Sept 1974, 5.

32. *Back to the Movement*, vol. 14, Eyes on the Prize, prod. and dir. Davis Lacy, Jr. & James Devinney, 60 min., 1990, videocassette, 18:15; Lori B. Andrews, *Black Power, White Blood: The Life and Times of Johnny Spain* (New York: Pantheon Books, 1996), 88.

33. *Report of the National Advisory Commission on Civil Disorders*, 5, 299.

34. Ibid., 302.

35. National Center on Police and Community Relations, *A National Survey of Police and Community Relations* (East Lansing: Michigan State University Press, 1967), 148, 155.

36. *Ain't Gonna Shuffle No More*, vol. 11, Eyes on the Prize, prod. and dir. Sam Pollard & Sheila Bernard, 60 min., 1990, videocassette, 29:00; *Greater Milwaukee Star*, 23 May 1970, 1.

37. Editorial, "The Police and the Negro Community," *Crisis* (August-Sept 1968), 223, "White Tigers vs. Black Panthers," *Crisis* (Oct 1968), 276.

38. *UWM Post*, 28 Feb 1969, 1.

39. Ralph Knoohuizen, Richard P. Fahey & Deborah J. Palmer, *Police and Their Use of Fatal Force in Chicago* (Chicago: 1972), 20.

40. *Los Angeles Times*, 14 Jan 1972, part 2, 1.

41. Newton, *Revolutionary Suicide*, 110.

42. Fanon, 38.

43. Hilliard & Cole, 140.

44. Newton, *Revolutionary Suicide*, 138–140; Bobby Seale, *Seize the Time: The Story of the Black Panther Party and Huey Newton* (Random House, 1970: reprint, Baltimore: Black Classic Press, 1991), 135; Newton, "War Against the Panthers," 40.

45. Newton, *Revolutionary Suicide*, 138–140.

46. Newton, *Revolutionary Suicide*, 120.

47. Earl Anthony, *Picking up the Gun: A Report on the Black Panthers* (New York: The Dial Press, 1970), 37.

48. *Black Panther*, 12–18 April 1968, 3.

49. "The Police Versus the Black Panthers," 23; *UWM Post*, 3 Dec 1971, 6; *Los Angeles Times*, 17 Mar 1972, part 1, 25; Roy Wilkins & Ramsey Clark, *Search and Destroy: A Report by the Commission of Inquiry* (New York: Metropolitan Research Center, Inc., 1973), 246; Federal Bureau of Investigation, SAC, Chicago, to Director, December 8, 1969, CG 44–1503.

50. *A Nation of Law?*, 27:00

51. *UWM Crossroads*, 29 Oct 1970, 10.
52. Wilkins and Clark, 3, 38, 246.
53. Kenneth O'Reilly, *Racial Matters: The FBI's Secret File on Black America* (New York: The Free Press, 1989), 311; *A Nation of Law?* , 32:45; *Berkeley Barb*, 19–26 Jan 1968, 5.
54. *Power!*, 22:00.
55. William Lee Brent, *Long Time Gone* (New York: Times Books, 1996), 91, 124; *Black Panther*, 7 Feb 1970, 3; Congress, House, Committee on Internal Security, *Black Panther Party, part one, Investigation of Kansas City Chapter; National Organization Data: Hearings before the Committee on Internal Security*, 91st Cong., 2nd sess., 4, 5, 6, 10 Mar 1970, 2683.
56. Senate Select Committee on Nutrition and Human Needs, *Hunger in the Classroom: Then and Now*, report prepared by George McGovern, 92nd Cong., 2nd sess., 1972, iii.
57. *Black Panther*, 16 Oct 1976, G.
58. *Black Panther*, 27 Apr 1969, 10–11.
59. Citizens Board of Inquiry into Hunger and Malnutrition in the United States, *Hunger U.S.A Revisited* (n.d), 10–12.
60. Ernest F. Hollings, *The Case Against Hunger: A Demand for National Policy* (New York: Cowles Book Co., 1970), 1, 3; *Milwaukee Courier*, 2 Sept 1972, 1; *Milwaukee Courier*, 30 Sept 1972, 3.
61. *A Nation of Law?*, 10:30.
62. *Black Panther*, 6 Sept 1969; *Black Panther*, 4 Jan 1969, 16; *Black Panther*, 27 Apr 1969, 3; *Black Panther*, 14 Dec 1968, 15; G. Louis Heath, *Off the Pigs!: The History and Literature of the Black Panther Party* (Metuchen, NJ: The Scarecrow Press, 1976), 86.
63. Ollie Johnson, III, "Explaining the Demise o1 the Black Panther Party: The Role of Internal Factors," in *The Black Panther Party: Reconsidered*, 401; *Black Panther*, 5 July 1969, 15; *Black Panther*, 13 Sept 1969, 6, 19; *Black Panther Party, part one, Investigation of Kansas City Chapter; National Organization Data*, 2693; Seale, 413; Akua Njeri, *My Life with The Black Panther Party* (Oakland: Burning Spear, 1991), 11; Jimerson; Heath, *Off the Pigs!*, 99; G. Louis Heath, *The Black Panther Leaders Speak* (Metuchen, NJ: Scarecrow Press, 1976), 125, *UWM Post*, 14 Apr 1972, 2.
64. Seale, 380.
65. Jimerson.
66. Congress, House, Committee on Internal Security, *Black Panther Party, part two, Investigation of Seattle Chapter: Hearings before the Committee on Internal Security*, 91st cong., 2d sess., 12, 13, 14, 20 May 1970, 4352.
67. Terry Cannon, *All Power to the People: The Story of the Black Panther Party* (San Francisco: Peoples Free Press, 1970), 35.
68. Max Seham, *Black and American Medical Care* (Minneapolis: University of Minnesota Press, 1973), 115; Pierre de Vise, *Misused and Misplaced Hospitals and Doctors: A Locational Analysis of the Urban Health Crisis* (Washington D.C.: 1973), 1.

69. *Black Panther*, 18 Oct 1969, 3.
70. Heath, *The Black Panther Leaders Speak*, 125; Heath, *Off the Pigs!*, 98; *Black Panther*, 30 Aug 1969, 16; *Black Panther Party, part one, Investigation of Kansas City Chapter; National Organization Data*, 2638; Newton, "War Against the Panthers," 93.
71. Brown, 276; *UWM Post*, 14 Apr 1972, 2; Hilliard and Cole, 339; *The New York Times*, 5 Oct 1969, 66; *The Bugle American* (Milwaukee), 2–9 Feb 1972, 4, 5; Dick Campbell, "Sickle-Cell Anemia and Its Effect on Black People," *Crisis* (Jan-Feb 1971), 7.
72. Njeri, 11.
73. Kenneth Clark, ed. *Racism and American Education: A Dialogue and Agenda for Action*, with a foreword by Averell Harriman, and an introduction by McGeorge Bundy (New York: Harper & Row, 1970), 151.
74. *Milwaukee Courier*, 8 Sept 1973, 4
75. Newton, *Revolutionary Suicide*, 22; Seale, 416–417.
76. *Black Panther*, 12 July 1969, 3; *Baltimore Free Press*, 1 Oct 1968, 5.
77. *Black Panther*, 9 Aug 1969, 19, 21; *Black Panther*, 13 Sept 1969, 8; *Black Panther Party, part one, Investigation of Kansas City Chapter; National Organization Data*, 2807; *Black Panther*, 30 Aug 1969, 21; *Black Panther*, 12 July 1969, 3; JoNina Abron, "Serving the People: The Survival Programs of the Black Panther Party," in *The Black Panther Party: Reconsidered*, 186.
78. Newton, *Revolutionary Suicide*, 71.
79. *The Black Panther*, 15 Nov 1970, 14; Hilliard and Cole, 210; *Berkeley Barb*, 8–14 Mar 1968, 5.
80. Leo Carroll, Hacks, *Blacks and Cons: Race Relations in a Maximum Security Prison* (Lexington, KY: Lexington Books, 1974), xi.
81. *In Search of Common Ground*, (New York: W. W. & Norton & Company, Inc., 1973), 87; Newton, *Revolutionary Suicide*, 116–118; Fultz.
82. *Power!*, 31:50; Brown, 321; *UWM Post*, 9 Mar 1973, 1; Van Deburg, 160; Jimerson.
83. Pearson, 128; Heath, *The Black Panther Leaders Speak*, x; DeLoach, 289; Newton, *Revolutionary Suicide*, 142; *Black Panther*, 9 May 1970, 10; *Black Panther Party, part one, Investigation of Kansas City Chapter; National Organization Data*, 2698; Jones and Jeffries, in *The Black Panther Party: Reconsidered*, 29.
84. *Black Panther*, 18 Oct 1969, 12; *Black Panther*, 4 Oct 1969, 12; Jimerson; *Black Panther Party, part two, Investigation of Seattle Chapter*, 4303; Seale, 417; *Black Panther*, 6 Sept 1969, 19; *Black Panther*, 11 Oct 1969, 5.
85. Chevigny, 68; *Black Panther*, 22 Nov 1969, 15.
86. Seale, 235, 270.
87. Brown, 276; *Milwaukee Courier*, 23 Jan 1971, 2; Seale, 415; Van Deburg, 160; Newton, *Revolutionary Suicide*, 121; *UWM Post*, 14 Apr 1972, 2; *Milwaukee Courier*, 14 August 1971, 2; *UWM Post*, 9 Mar 1973, 1.

88. Brown, 335; Chevigny, 79; Heath, *Off the Pigs!*, 85.

NOTES TO CHAPTER THREE

1. Alice Smith, *The History of Wisconsin, From Exploration to Statehood* (Madison: State Historical Society of Wisconsin, 1973), 13, 113.
2. Ibid., 163.
3. Ibid., 143–144.
4. *The Thirteenth Census of the United States*, 1910, vol. 3 (Washington D.C.: Government Printing Office, 1913), 1049, 1073; Joe Trotter, *Black Milwaukee: The Making of an Industrial Proletariat, 1915–1945* (Urbana: University of Illinois Press, 1985), 4.
5. *Census*, 1090.
6. Neil McMillen, *Dark Journey: Black Mississippians in the Age of Jim Crow* (Urbana: University of Illinois Press, 1989; 262–263); Arwin Smallwood, *The Atlas of African American History and Politics: From the Slave Trade to Modern Times* (Boston: McGraw-Hill, 1998), 111, 124; Trotter, 39; The Great Migration occurred primarily between 1914–1929, as hundreds of thousands of African Americans left the rural south mainly for the urban north.
7. *The Fourteenth Census of the United States*, 1920, vol. 3 (Washington D.C.: Government Printing Office, 1923), 1128.
8. *The Sixteenth Census of the United States*, 1940, vol. 2, part 7 (Washington D.C.: Government Printing Office, 1943), 640.
9. Frank Aukofer, *City with a Chance* (Milwaukee: The Bruce Publishing Company, 1968), 34–35.
10. *The Seventeenth Census of the United States*, 1950, vol. 2, part 49 (Washington D.C.: Government Printing Office, 1952), 49–9, 49–57.
11. *The Eighteenth Census of the United States*, 1960, vol. 1, part 51 (Washington D.C.: Government Printing Office, 1962), 51–26; School of Social Work, University of Wisconsin-Madison, *Social Problem Indicators and Related Demographic Characteristics, Milwaukee* (Madison: University of Wisconsin-Madison, 1966), 4.
12. *US Census*, 1128; *The Fifteenth Census of the United States*, 1930 (Washington D.C.: Government Printing Office, 1932), 1333; *The Nineteenth Census of the United States*, 1970 (Washington D.C.: Government Printing Office, 1973), 51–15, 51–72.
13. Joe McClain, former President of the NAACP Youth Commandos, interview by author, 6 May 2005, tape in possession of author.
14. McClain.
15. Peter K. Eisinger, *Patterns of Interracial Politics: Conflict and Cooperation in the City* (New York: Academic Press, 1976), 34; School of Social Work, 2.
16. Aukofer, 37.
17. Ibid., 35.

18. Mark Braun, "Social Change and the Empowerment of the Poor: Poverty Representation" (Ph.D. diss., University of Wisconsin-Milwaukee, 1999), 43.

19. Aukofer, 10.

20. Martin Gruberg, *A Case Study in US Urban Leadership: The Incumbency of Milwaukee Mayor Henry Maier* (Aldershot, England: Avebury, 1996), 161; Henry Maier, *The Mayor Who Made Milwaukee Famous* (Lanham, Maryland: Madison Books, 1993), 94–95.

21. McClain.

22. Ronald Snyder, "Chief for Life: Harold Breier and his Era" (PhD diss, University of Wisconsin-Milwaukee, 2002), 48–50.

23. Snyder, 26; Illustrating the widespread corruption on the Milwaukee Police Department during the early 1960s, 35 officers retired or resigned, and 6 were brought up on criminal charges, as a result of a 1962 internal investigation.

24. Ibid., 25, 37.

25. Braun, 63.

26. Ad Hoc Committee on Police Administration in Milwaukee (1968), Milwaukee Small Collection 177, University of Wisconsin-Milwaukee archives, Milwaukee, WI.

27. *Milwaukee Sentinel*, 12 June 1969, 16.

28. *Kaleidoscope* (Milwaukee), Jan 17-Feb 13 1969, 1.

29. Braun, 72.

30. *Greater Milwaukee Star*, 15 Apr 1967, 1; *Greater Milwaukee Star*, 22 Apr 1967, 1, 5; *Greater Milwaukee Star*, 6 May 1967, 1; *Greater Milwaukee Star*, 1 July 1967, 1.

31. Henry J. Schmandt, John G. Goldback & Donald B. Vogel, *Milwaukee: A Contemporary Urban Profile* (New York: Praeger Publishers, 1971), 155.

32. *Greater Milwaukee Star*, 5 Oct 1968, 4.

33. Braun, 53, Henry J. Schmandt & Harold M. Rose, *Citizen Attitudes in Milwaukee: A Further Look* (Milwaukee: Milwaukee Urban Observatory, 1972), 170; 1967 witnessed over 125 civil disorders throughout the nation.

34. Aukofer, 12–13.

35. *Greater Milwaukee Star*, 29 Apr 1967, 3; *Greater Milwaukee Star*, 13 May 1967, 1.

36. *Greater Milwaukee Star*, 29, Apr 1967, 3.

37. Ibid.

38. Ad Hoc Committee on Police Administration in Milwaukee.

39. Karl H. Flaming, *Who 'Riots' and Why?* (Milwaukee: Milwaukee Urban League, 1968), vii, xi, 2, 46.

40. Ad Hoc Committee on Police Administration in Milwaukee (1968).

41. *UWM Post*, 17 May 1968, 10.

42. Coleman, 12.

43. *UWM Crossroads*, 19 Nov 1970, 2.

44. Braun, 24; Schmandt & Rose, 1, 18, 39, 50.

45. *Bugle American*, 26–3 April-May 1972, 7

46. Karl H. Flaming, John Ong, *A Social Report for Milwaukee: Trends and Indicators* (Milwaukee: Milwaukee Urban Observatory, 1973), v.

47. *UWM Post*, 1 Oct 1974, 5.

48. *Milwaukee Courier*, 4 Oct 1969, 1; *Milwaukee Courier*, 31 Jan 1970, 1; *Milwaukee Star*, 9 Oct 1971, 1; *Milwaukee Star*, 23 Oct 1971, 1; *Milwaukee Star-Times*, 4 Feb 1973, 1.

49. *UWM Post*, 14 Feb 1973, 4.

50. *Milwaukee Courier*, 8 Jan 1977, 1; *Milwaukee Star*, 3 Jan 1970, 5.

51. *Milwaukee Courier*, 22 Sept 1973, 3; *Milwaukee Courier*, 30 Aug 1975, 1.

52. Snyder, 80–81. In 1979, Louis Krause, a retired member of the Milwaukee police force, alleged that he and Officer Thomas Grady had placed a knife on Bell's person after Grady had shot and killed Bell. An investigation was demanded by both Mayor Maier and the Milwaukee Common Council, but Breier ignored their pleas and no one could force him to conduct an investigation because a 1911 law gave lifetime tenure to the Chief of Police.

53. *Milwaukee Star*, 13 Jan 1968, 1; *Milwaukee Star*, 2 Mar 1968, 4: *Milwaukee Star*, 17 Feb 1968, 4; *Milwaukee Star*, 9 Mar 1968, 4; *Milwaukee Sentinel*, 12 June 1969, 16; *Milwaukee Courier*, 14 Apr 1973, 8; *UWM Post*, 30 Apr 1971, 16; *UWM Post*, 16 Jan 1968, 9; *Milwaukee Courier*, 10 July 1971, 1.

54. Ad Hoc Committee on Police Administration in Milwaukee.

55. *Milwaukee Star*, 13 Jan 1968, 1; *Milwaukee Star*, 2 Mar 1968, 4: *Milwaukee Star*, 17 Feb 1968, 4; *Milwaukee Star*, 9 Mar 1968, 4; *Milwaukee Sentinel*, 12 June 1969, 16; *Milwaukee Courier*, 14 Apr 1973, 8; *UWM Post*, 30 Apr 1971, 16; *UWM Post*, 16 Jan 1968, 9; *Milwaukee Courier*, 10 July 1971, 1.

56. National Association for the Advancement of Colored People (NAACP) Records, Milwaukee Manuscript Collection EP, Box 7, Folder 8, University of Wisconsin-Milwaukee Archives.

57. Milwaukee Urban League, Records 1919–1979, Milwaukee Manuscript Collection EZ; NAACP Records, Box 8, Folder 20.

58. NAACP Records, Box 5, Folders 1 and 15.

59. Congress of Racial Equality (CORE) Records, Milwaukee Manuscript Collection 27, Box 1, Folder 6, University of Wisconsin-Milwaukee Archives.

60. Aukofer, 39–40.

61. Ibid., 40.

62. Ibid., 40.

63. CORE Records, Box 1, Folders 4 and 6.

64. Braun, 32.

65. Jay Wendelberger, "The Open Housing Movement in Milwaukee: Hidden Transcripts of the Urban Poor" (MA thesis, University of Wisconsin-Milwaukee, 1996), 16.

66. Lloyd Barbee, Milwaukee Manuscript Collection 16, Box 22, Folder 3, University of Wisconsin-Milwaukee Archives; Wendelberger, 26–27.

67. Wendelberger, 29–31.

68. McClain; Wendelberger, 26.
69. NAACP Records, Box 5, folder 15; Wendelberger 2, 26, 35–36. The Eagle's Club was a social club in Milwaukee that boasted a membership that included local judges and influential businesspeople.
70. McClain.
71. Barbee, Box 22, Folder 10; Wendelberger, 48–49, 58; McClain.
72. McClain.
73. Ibid.
74. *"Freedom News." Crisis* (NAACP) 74, no. 10 (1967): 492.
75. James Groppi, Box 16, Folder 1, Milwaukee Manuscript Collection, University of Wisconsin-Milwaukee Archives; Wendelberger, 84–87, 107.
76. Ollie Johnson, in *The Black Panther Party: Reconsidered,* 393; Johnson identifies 1968–1970 as the "peak years" of the Party. According to Johnson, Black Power organizations became much more appealing in the wake of the assassination of Martin Luther King, Jr. in 1968, and the Panthers also became more well-known following the widely publicized imprisonment of Huey Newton in 1967, and the killing of Bobby Hutton, one of the first members of the Party.
77. *Milwaukee Sentinel,* June 12, 1969, 16; Miriam White, "The Black Panther's Free Breakfast for Children Program" (M.A. thesis, University of Wisconsin-Madison, 1988), 84.
78. *Milwaukee Star,* July 18, 1970, 5; *Milwaukee Courier,* Feb 7, 1970, 3; *Milwaukee Courier,* Sept 27, 1969, 8; White, 16.
79. FBI, SAC, Milwaukee, to Director, January 24, 1969, 105-HQ-165706–30; FBI, SAC Milwaukee to Director, February 12, 1969, 105-HQ-165706–30; FBI, SAC Milwaukee to Director, April 25, 1969, 105-HQ-165706–30.
80. FBI, SAC Milwaukee, to Director, April 25, 1969, 105-HQ-165706–30; *Milwaukee Journal,* 23 Mar 1969, part 2, 1; *Milwaukee Courier,* 30 Mar 1974, 1; *Milwaukee Journal,* 19 June 1969, 1; *Milwaukee Sentinel,* 12 June 1969, 5, 16; *Milwaukee Sentinel,* 23 Oct 1969, 14;
81. FBI, SAC Milwaukee to Director, April 25, 1969, 105-HQ-165706–30.
82. *Milwaukee Sentinel,* 12 June 1969, 16.
83. *Milwaukee Courier,* 14 June 1969, section 2, 8.
84. *Milwaukee Journal,* 23 March 1969, part 2, 8.
85. Ibid.
86. FBI, SAC, location not specified, to SAC Milwaukee, May 13, 1969, 105-HQ-165706–30.
87. *Milwaukee Courier,* 17 May 1969, 1.
88. McClain.
89. FBI, Milwaukee to Director, June 17, 1969, 105-HQ-165706–30; FBI, SAC Milwaukee to Director, June 18, 1969, 105-HQ-165706–30.
90. *Milwaukee Courier,* 6 Dec 1969, 4.
91. *Milwaukee Courier,* 1 Mar 1969, 2.
92. *Milwaukee Courier,* 14 June 1969, 1, sect. 2, 8.
93. *Milwaukee Journal,* 19 June 1969, 1, 3; *Milwaukee Journal,* 23 Oct 1969, 3; FBI, SAC Milwaukee, to Director, June 18, 1969, 105-HQ-165706–30.
94. *Milwaukee Star,* 27 Sept 1969, 1, 4; *Milwaukee Courier,* 27 Sept, 1969, 1.

95. *Milwaukee Journal*, 22 Sept 1969, 1, part 2; *Milwaukee Courier*, 27 Sept 1969, 6.
96. *Milwaukee Courier*, 30 1974, 18.
97. *Milwaukee Courier*, 27 Sept 1969, 1.
98. *Milwaukee Courier*, 27 Sept 1969, 8.
99. *Greater Milwaukee Star*, 14 Aug 1971, 6; *Milwaukee Sentinel*, 5 Feb 1973, 5; Black Panther Party, Social Action Vertical File, MS-577, Box 6.
100. *Milwaukee Sentinel*, 23 Oct 1969, 14.
101. FBI, SAC, Milwaukee, to Director, April 25, 1969, 105-HQ-165706–30.
102. FBI, SAC Milwaukee, to Director, May 27, 1969, 105-HQ-165706–30.
103. *Milwaukee Sentinel*, 26 Nov 1969, 8; The Party's Central Committee was the main decision making body of the Party at the national level, consisting of roughly 10–15 individuals, including Huey Newton and Bobby Seale.
104. *Milwaukee Courier*, 30 Mar 1974, 18.
105. *Greater Milwaukee Star*, 27 Apr 1972, 1.
106. *Milwaukee Courier*, 30 Mar 1974, 18; *Milwaukee Star-Times*, 29 June 1972, 4.
107. Black Panther Party Clippings File, Milwaukee Public Library.
108. *Milwaukee Courier*, Mar 30, 1974, 1, 18.
109. Jones & Jeffries, 34–35, point out that women made up a significant percentage of Party members; McGee.
110. McGee.
111. *Milwaukee Courier*, 14 June 1969, section 2, 8; McGee.
112. McGee.
113. McGee.
114. Ibid.
115. Ibid.
116. Ibid.
117. The internal dissension is discussed in chapter six; the chapter that analyzes the various flaws of the Party.

NOTES TO CHAPTER FOUR

1. Henry Maier, University of Wisconsin-Manuscript Collection, Box 9, Folder 24, University of Wisconsin-Milwaukee Archives.
2. Barbee, Box 55, Folder 4.
3. Barbee, Box 55, Folder 4; *Milwaukee Courier*, 20 July 1974, 1.
4. *Milwaukee Journal*, 13 Oct 1969, part 2, 9.
5. Ibid.
6. *Milwaukee Courier*, 2 Aug 1969, 1, 10.
7. *Milwaukee Journal*, 13 Oct 1969, 9.
8. *Milwaukee Courier*, 2 Aug 1969, 10.
9. *Milwaukee Journal*, 13 Oct 1969, 9.
10. *Milwaukee Courier*, 2 Aug 1969, 1, 10.
11. *Milwaukee Courier*, 2 Aug 1969, 1, 10.

12. Floyd Hayes, III & Francis Kiene, III, "All Power to the People': The Political Thought of Huey P. Newton and the Black Panther Party," in *The Black Panther Party: Reconsidered*, 167; *Milwaukee Courier* 17 Jan 1970, 8; *Greater Milwaukee Star*, 26 July 1969, 2.

13. Social Action Vertical File, MSS 577, Box 56, Wisconsin Committee to Combat Fascism Folder.

14. Ibid.

15. Ibid.

16. *Milwaukee Courier*, 20 July 1974, 4.

17. Black Panther Party Clippings File.

18. Ibid.

19. Ibid.

20. Ibid.

21. *Milwaukee Courier*, 11 May 1974, 3; *Milwaukee Courier*, 20 July 1974, 4.

22. *Milwaukee Courier*, 16 Apr 1977, 1, 11; Wisconsin State Legislative Reference Bureau, 608–266–0341; Governor Pat Lucey was in China at this time, therefore Martin Schreiber was the acting governor.

23. Snyder, 8.

24. Snyder, 8–9.

25. *Milwaukee Courier*, 2 Sept 1972, 1.

26. Social Action Vertical File, MSS 577, Box 40, People's Committee for Survival folder.

27. Social Action Vertical File, MSS 577, Box 40, People's Committee for Survival folder; *Milwaukee Courier*, 2 Sept 1972, 1.

28. *Milwaukee Courier*, 2 Sept 1972, 1, 7.

29. *Milwaukee Courier*, July 15, 1972, 1; *Black Panther*, Mar 23, 1974, 3; *Milwaukee Courier*, Sept 2, 1972, 1, 7; *Milwaukee Courier*, Mar 30, 1974, 1, 18; *Milwaukee Courier*, July 10, 1976, 14; McGee.

30. Barbee, Box 56, Folder 22.

31. Barbee, Box 56, Folder 22.

32. Social Action Vertical File, MSS 577, Box 40, People's Committee for Survival folder.

33. McGee.

34. *Milwaukee Courier*, July 10, 1976, 14.

35. *Milwaukee Courier*, 2 Sept 1972, 1; *Milwaukee Courier*, 28 Aug 1972, 1

36. *Milwaukee Courier*, 14 Aug 1971, 1; *Milwaukee Courier*, 28 Aug 1971, 1; *Milwaukee Courier*, 12 Aug 1972, 1; *Milwaukee Courier*, 4 Jan 1975, 4.

37. *Milwaukee Courier*, 4 Jan 1975, 4.

38. *Greater Milwaukee Star*, 13 Sept 1969, 21.

39. *Milwaukee Star-Times*, 23 Nov 1972, 1.

40. *Black Panther*, 16 June 1975, 2.

41. *Black Panther*, 16 June 1975, 2.

42. *Milwaukee Courier*, 29 Nov 1975, 1, 14; McGee.

43. *Milwaukee Courier*, 29 June 1975, 9.
44. *Milwaukee Courier*, 29 Nov 1975, 14.
45. *Milwaukee Courier*, 17 Jan 1976, 3.
46. Ibid.
47. *Milwaukee Courier*, 29 Nov 1975, 14.
48. Edwin Clarke & Steve Paulson introduction by Belden Paulson, *The Harambee Health Experiment* (University of Wisconsin-Extension: Center for Urban Community Development, 1983), 8.
49. Clarke & Paulson, 9.
50. Clarke & Paulson, 12, 19; McGee; The name "Harambee" was chosen because it is the name of the neighborhood where the People's Free Health Center was located.
51. Clarke & Paulson, 38.
52. *Milwaukee Sentinel*, 12 June 1969, 16.
53. *Milwaukee Star*, 7 June 1969, 18; *Milwaukee Star*, 21 June 1969, 1, 5; *Milwaukee Sentinel*, 12 June 1969, 16.
54. *Kaleidoscope* (Milwaukee) June 20-July 3, 1969, 3; *Greater Milwaukee Star*, 21 June 1969, 5.
55. *Milwaukee Sentinel*, 9 June 1969, part 2, 11.
56. *Milwaukee Journal*, 10 June 1969, part 2, 2; *Milwaukee Sentinel*, 9 June 1969, part 2, 11.
57. *Milwaukee Courier*, 12 June 1969, 1.
58. *Milwaukee Sentinel*, 30 June 1969, part 1, 5.
59. *Milwaukee Courier*, 30 March 1974, 18.
60. McGee.
61. *Milwaukee Courier*, 30 Mar 1974, 18; *Black Panther*, 29 Sept 1973, 5; *Milwaukee Star*, 13 Sept 1969, 21; *Black Panther*, 18 May 1974, 5.
62. *Greater Milwaukee Star*, 13 Sept 1969, 21.
63. *Milwaukee Courier*, 30 March 1974, 18.
64. Barbee, box 57, folder 1; *Black Panther*, 28 Dec 1974, 5; *Black Panther*, 1 Mar 1975, 8.
65. Barbee, box 57, folder 1; *Black Panther*, 5 May 1975, 8.
66. *Black Panther*, 11 Aug 1975, 5.
67. *Black Panther*, 23 June 1975, 5.
68. [68]*Black Panther*, 12 Apr 1975, 5.
69. Ibid.
70. *Milwaukee Star-Times*, 18 Mar 1976, 1.
71. *Black Panther*, 12 Apr 1975, 5; *Black Panther*, 24 Sept 1977, 1.
72. *Milwaukee Star-Times*, 1 June 1972, 3.
73. *Black Panther*, 31 July 1976, 10.
74. Ibid.
75. *Milwaukee Courier*, 30 Mar 1974, 1, 18.
76. *Milwaukee Courier*, June 14, 1969, 1; *Milwaukee Courier*, Aug 16, 1969, 1; *Milwaukee Courier*, July 10, 1976, 1, 14; *Milwaukee Courier*, Mar 30, 1974, 18, *Milwaukee Sentinel*, Apr 7, 1973, part 2, 15; White, 86–87.
77. *Milwaukee Courier*, Mar 30, 1974, 18.

78. McGee.
79. *Milwaukee Courier*, 30 March 1974, 1, 18.
80. McGee.
81. Ibid.
82. Ibid.; It was called "canning," because Panther members held out a can for people to deposit money into.
83. McGee.
84. *Milwaukee Courier*, 30 Mar 1974, 18.
85. *UWM Post*, 26 Sept 1969, 7.
86. FBI, SAC, Milwaukee, to Director, June 18, 1969, 105-HQ-165706–30.
87. *Milwaukee Courier*, 10 July 1976, 1, 14.

NOTES TO CHAPTER FIVE

1. *Greater Milwaukee Star*, 21 June 1969, 1.
2. www.hungertaskforce.org/index.htm; *Milwaukee Courier*, 4 July 1970, 1, 5; Social Development Commission, *Children in Poverty: The State of Milwaukee's Children*, (Milwaukee, n.d.), 12.
3. Hunger Task Force of Milwaukee, University of Wisconsin-Milwaukee Collection, Box 1, Folder 17, University of Wisconsin-Milwaukee Archives.
4. *Milwaukee Journal*, 30 July 1969, 2.
5. *Greater Milwaukee Star*, 7 June 1969, 5.
6. *Milwaukee Sentinel*, 23 May 1969, 20.
7. *Milwaukee Sentinel*, 30 July 1969, 8.
8. Social Action Vertical File, MSS 577, Box 6, Black Panther Party Folder.
9. *Milwaukee Courier*, 17 May 1969, 1.
10. *Milwaukee Sentinel*, 23 May 1969, 20.
11. Ibid.
12. *Greater Milwaukee Star*, 7 June 1969, 5.
13. *Milwaukee Courier*, 14 June 1969, section 2, 8.
14. Ibid.; Crayton resigned from his role at the church for what he called "personal reasons."
15. *Milwaukee Courier*, 21 June 1969, 6.
16. Reverend Joseph Ellwanger, telephone interview with author, 23 June 1999; Social Action Vertical File, MSS 577, Box 6, Black Panther Party Folder; *Milwaukee Star*, 27 Sept 1969, 4; *Black Panther*, 5 July 1969, 15; *Milwaukee Courier*, 21 June 1969, 1.
17. *Milwaukee Journal*, 18 June 1969, 1.
18. Ellwanger.
19. Ibid.
20. *Milwaukee Journal*, 30 July 1969, 2.
21. *Milwaukee Courier*, 21 June 1969, 1.
22. *Milwaukee Courier*, 21 June 1969, 6.
23. *Black Panther*, 5 July 1969, 15; *Milwaukee Courier*, 21 June 1969, 1.
24. *Milwaukee Journal*, 18 June 1969, 1, 22; *Milwaukee Courier*, 21 June 1969, 1.

25. *Milwaukee Journal*, 18 June 1969, 1.
26. *Milwaukee Courier*, 12 July 1969, 1; *Milwaukee Journal*, 18 June 1969, 1, 22; *Milwaukee Courier*, 21 June 1969, 6.
27. *Milwaukee Courier*, 21 June 1969, 4.
28. *Milwaukee Journal*, 18 June 1969, 22.
29. *Milwaukee Courier*, 12 July 1969, 1; FBI, SAC, Milwaukee, to Director, June 18, 1969, 105-HQ-165706–30.
30. FBI, SAC, Milwaukee, to Director, June 18, 1969, 105-HQ-165706–30.
31. *Milwaukee Journal*, 18 June 1969, 22.
32. Henry Maier, Box 9, Folder 24.
33. *Milwaukee Journal*, 30 July 1969, 2.
34. Ibid.
35. *Greater Milwaukee Star*, 30 Aug 1969, 2.
36. Ellwanger.
37. *Milwaukee Sentinel*, 30 July 1969, 8.
38. *Milwaukee Courier*, 30 August 1969, 1.
39. Ibid.
40. Ibid.
41. *Greater Milwaukee Star*, 6 Sept 1969, 4.
42. *Milwaukee Courier*, 4 July 1970, 1.
43. *Milwaukee Courier*, 4 July 1970, 1.
44. Miriam White, 96; Hunger Task Force, Box 1, Folder 3; Ellwanger.
45. *Milwaukee Courier*, 4 July 1970, 1.
46. *Milwaukee Courier*, 4 July 1970, 6.
47. Hunger Task Force, Box 1, Folder 3; *Milwaukee Courier*, 30 Sept 1972, 3.
48. Social Action Vertical File, MSS 577, Box 40, People's Committee for Survival Folder; *UWM Post Magazine*, Nov 1973, 1; White, 85; *Milwaukee Sentinel*, 5 Feb 1973, 5; *Milwaukee Courier*, 30 Mar 1974, 18; McGee.
49. People's Committee for Survival, Social Action Vertical File, MSS 577, box 40; *UWM Post Magazine*, Nov 1973, 1; *Milwaukee Sentinel*, 5 Feb 1973, 5; *Milwaukee Courier*, 30 Mar 1974, 18; McGee.
50. *UWM Post Magazine*, Nov 1973, 1.
51. McGee.
52. *UWM Post Magazine*, Nov 1973, 1.
53. McGee.
54. Social Action Vertical File, MSS 577, Box 40, People's Committee for Survival Folder; *UWM Post Magazine*, Nov 1973, 1; White, 85; *Milwaukee Sentinel*, 5 Feb 1973, 5; *Milwaukee Courier*, 30 Mar 1974, 18.
55. McGee; The Party's dissolution is discussed in greater detail in Chapter Three.
56. White, 96; Hunger Task Force, Box 1, Folder 3; Ellwanger.
57. *Milwaukee Courier*, 6 Dec 1975, 13.
58. *Milwaukee Courier*, 1 Nov 1975, 1, 4.
59. *Milwaukee Courier*, 1 Nov 1975, 4.
60. Ibid.
61. Ibid.

62. *Milwaukee Courier*, 1 Nov 1975, 1, 4; *Milwaukee Courier*, 29 Nov 1975, 1, 14; *Milwaukee Courier*, 6 Dec 1975, 1, 13; *Milwaukee Courier*, 8 Nov 1975, 1, 6.
63. Hunger Task Force, Box 1, Folder 2.
64. Ibid.
65. Ibid.
66. Hunger Task Force, Box 2, Folder 63; www.hungertaskforce.org/all_about.htm.
67. http://www.hungertaskforce.org/Bringing_Food/index.html
68. *Milwaukee Journal*, 23 May 1969, 25.
69. *Milwaukee Journal*, 18 June 1969, 22.
70. *Milwaukee Courier*, 21 June 1969, 6.

NOTES TO CHAPTER SIX

1. These works are discussed in much greater detail in the introduction.
2. *Milwaukee Courier*, 24 Jan 1970, 3; *Milwaukee Courier*, 17 Jan 1970, 1.
3. *Milwaukee Courier*, 17 Jan 1970, 1.
4. *Milwaukee Courier*, 20 Dec 1969, 1
5. *Milwaukee Courier*, 13 Apr 1974, 3; *Milwaukee Journal*, 26 Nov 1969, 1
6. *Milwaukee Sentinel*, 26 Nov 1969, 1.
7. McClain.
8. *Milwaukee Courier*, 20 Dec 1969, 1.
9. *Milwaukee Courier*, 24 Jan 1970, 3.
10. *Milwaukee Courier*, 20 Dec 1969, 1.
11. *Milwaukee Courier*, 17 Jan 1970, 1.
12. *Milwaukee Courier*, 17 Jan 1970, 8.
13. *Milwaukee Courier*, 17 Jan 1970, 8.
14. FBI, SAC, Milwaukee, to Director, June 18, 1969, 105-HQ-165706–30.
15. *Milwaukee Courier*, 24 Jan 1970, 3.
16. Ibid.
17. McClain.
18. Ibid.
19. SAC, Milwaukee, May 29, 1969, 105-HQ-165706–30.
20. *Milwaukee Courier*, 13 Apr 1974, 3; FBI, SAC, Milwaukee, to Director, June 3, 1969, 105-HQ-165706–30.
21. FBI, SAC, Milwaukee, May 29, 1969, 105-HQ-165706–30.
22. FBI, SAC, Milwaukee, to Director, June 13, 1969, 105-HQ-165706–30; FBI, SAC, Milwaukee to Director, August 18, 1969, 105-HQ-165706–30.
23. *Milwaukee Sentinel*, 26 Nov 1969, 8.
24. Ibid.
25. *Milwaukee Courier*, 17 Jan 1970, 1.
26. *Milwaukee Sentinel*, 26 Nov 1969, 8.
27. McClain.
28. *Milwaukee Sentinel*, 5 Feb 1973, 5; *Milwaukee Sentinel*, 26 Nov 1969, 1, 8.
29. McClain.

30. *Milwaukee Journal*, 23 March 1969, part 2, 8; *Milwaukee Sentinel*, 5 Feb 1973, 5; *Milwaukee Sentinel*, 26 Nov 1969, 1, 8; FBI, SAC, Milwaukee, to Director, April 25, 1969, 105-HQ-165706–30.
31. The disagreement is completely discussed in chapter 5.
32. *Milwaukee Sentinel*, 18 June 1969, 5.
33. *Black Panther*, 15 July 1969, 15.
34. *Greater Milwaukee Star*, 16 Aug 1969, 20; *Milwaukee Journal*, 11 Aug 1969, part 2, 2.
35. Jimerson.
36. Ellwanger.
37. *Milwaukee Journal*, 18 June 1969, 22.
38. *Milwaukee Courier*, 14 June 1969, 1.
39. Jones & Jeffries in *The Black Panther Party Reconsidered*, 44–45.
40. At the height of the Beatles popularity in the mid-1960s, Beatles' singer John Lennon stated that the Beatles were "more popular than Jesus Christ."
41. *Greater Milwaukee Star*, 16 Aug 1969, 20; *Milwaukee Journal*, 11 Aug 1969, part 2, 2.
42. McGee.
43. Ibid.
44. Ibid.
45. *Milwaukee Courier*, 7 June 1975, 4; *Milwaukee Courier*, 21 Feb 1976, 3.
46. *Milwaukee Courier*, 7 June 1975, 4; *Milwaukee Courier*, 21 Feb 1976, 3.
47. McGee
48. Ibid.
49. *Milwaukee Courier*, 17 Jan 1970, 1.

NOTES TO THE CONCLUSION

1. *Milwaukee Sentinel*, 12 June 1969, 5.
2. Consult pages 49–50 for a definition of "lumpenproletariat."
3. Chris Booker's "Lumpenization: A Critical Error of the Black Panther Party," in *The Black Panther Party: Reconsidered*, 337.
4. Sellers, 26, 37, 184–186, 194–196; *Kaleidoscope*, 4–17 July 1969, 4, 8; Wendelberger, 53–54, 82; *Radio Free Dixie*, 164–165.
5. Jones & Jeffries in *The Black Panther Party: Reconsidered*, 46.
6. White, 3.
7. *Milwaukee Courier*, 6 Dec 1969, 4.

NOTES TO THE EPILOGUE

1. www.jsonline.com/news/metro/may05/327952.asp
2. www.jsonline.com/news/metro/may05/327952.asp
3. www.jsonline.com/news/metro/mar05/313860.asp

4. www.jsonline.com/news/metro/may05/327952.asp
5. Ibid.
6. www.jsonline.com/new/metro/jun05/332631.asp
7. www.jsonline.com/news/editorials/feb05/304885.asp
8. www.jsonline.com/news/metro/may05/327952.asp
9. www.jsonline.com/news/metro/jun05/337007.asp
10. www.jsonline.com/news/metro/apr05/318760.asp
11. www.jsonline.com/news/metro/apr05/318760.asp
12. Liz Humphrey, Coordinator of Hunger Task Force Special Events. Phone message left by Humphrey on author's answering machine, 28 June 1999.
13. www.hungertaskforce.org/Graphics/Documents/htf_annual_report04.pdf

Bibliography

Primary sources

Manuscripts

Ad Hoc Committee on Police Administration in Milwaukee, Milwaukee Small Collection, UWM archives.

Barbee, Lloyd, Milwaukee Manuscript Collection, UWM archives.

Black Panther Party Clippings File, Milwaukee Public Library.

Black Panther Party, Social Action Vertical File, Wisconsin State Historical Society, Madison.

Coleman, Jonathan, UWM Manuscript Collection, UWM archives.

Congress of Racial Equality (CORE) Records, UWM archives.

Groppi, James, Milwaukee Manuscript Collection, UWM archives.

Hunger Task Force of Milwaukee, UWM Manuscript Collection, UWM archives.

Maier, Henry, UWM Manuscript Collection, UWM archives.

Milwaukee Urban League, Milwaukee Manuscript Collection, UWM archives.

National Association for the Advancement of Colored People Milwaukee Branch, Milwaukee Manuscript Collection, UWM archives.

People's Committee for Survival, Social Action Vertical File, Wisconsin State Historical Society, Madison.

Wisconsin Committee to Combat Fascism, Social Action Vertical File, Wisconsin State Historical Society, Madison.

Interviews

Ellwanger, Joseph, Reverend of Cross Lutheran Church, Milwaukee, Wi. Phone interview by author, 23 June 1999. Transcript in possession of author.

Fultz, Michael, former Black Panther. Interview by author, 16 Nov 1998. Madison. Transcript in possession of author.

McGee, Michael, former Black Panther. Interview by author, 15 Apr 2003. Milwaukee. Tape in possession of author.

McClain, Joe, former NAACP Youth Commando. Interview by author, 6 May 2005. Madison. Tape in possession of author.

Jimerson, Curtis R., former FBI agent. Telephone interview by author, 23 Nov 1997.

Government Documents

Deacons for Defense and Justice. Federal Bureau of Investigation Subject File. Obtained via the FBI's online database.

Milwaukee branch of the Black Panther Party. Federal Bureau of Investigation Subject File Obtained under the Freedom of Information Act.

The Thirteenth Census of the United States, 1910, vol. 3. Washington D.C.: Government Printing Office, 1913.

The Fourteenth Census of the United States, 1920, vol. 3. Washington D.C.: Government Printing Office, 1923.

The Fifteenth Census of the United States, 1930. Washington D.C.: Government Printing Office, 1932.

The Sixteenth Census of the United States, 1940, vol. 2, part 7. Washington D.C.: Government Printing Office, 1943.

The Seventeenth Census of the United States, 1950, vol. 2, part 49. Washington D.C.: Government Printing Office, 1952.

The Eighteenth Census of the United States, 1960, vol. 1, part 51. Washington D.C.: Government Printing Office, 1962.

The Nineteenth Census of the United States, 1970. Washington D.C.: Government Printing Office, 1973.

U.S. Congress. House. Committee on Internal Security. Black Panther Party, part one, Investigation of Kansas City Chapter; National Organization Data: Hearings before the Committee on Internal Security. 91st Cong., 2nd sess., 4, 5, 6 & 10 Mar 1970. U.S. Congress. House. Committee on Internal Security. Black Panther Party, part two, Investigation of Seattle Chapter: Hearings before the Committee on Internal Security. 91st Cong., 2nd sess., 12, 13, 14, & 20 May 1970.

U.S. Congress, Senate. Committee on Nutrition and Human Needs, Hunger in the Classroom: Then and Now, report prepared by George McGovern, 92nd sess., 2nd sess., 1972.

Newspapers

Baltimore Free Press
Berkeley Barb
Black Panther (Oakland)
Bugle American (Milwaukee)
Greater Milwaukee Star
Kaleidoscope (Milwaukee)
Los Angeles Times
Milwaukee Courier
Milwaukee Journal
Milwaukee Sentinel
Milwaukee Star-Times

New York Times
San Francisco Examiner
University of Wisconsin-Milwaukee (UWM) Courier
UWM Post
UWM Post Magazine

Books

Andrews, Lori B. *Black Power, White Blood: The Life and Times of Johnny Spain.* New York: Pantheon Books, 1996.

Anthony, Earl. *Picking Up the Gun: A Report on the Black Panthers.* New York: The Dial Press, 1970.

———. *Spitting in the Wind: The True Story Behind the Violent Legacy of the Black Panther Party.* Malibu, CA.: Roundtable Publishing Co., 1990.

Aptheker, Herbert, ed. *A Documentary History of Negro People in the United States.* Vol. 4, *From the New Deal to the End of World War II.* With a preface by William L. Patterson. New York: Citadel Press, 1974. Reprint, New York: Citadel Press, 1992.

———. ed. *A Documentary History of Negro People in the United States.* Vol. 7, *From the Alabama Protests to the Death of Martin Luther King, Jr.* With a foreword by Angela Y. Davis. New York: Citadel Press, 1994.

Aukofer, Frank. *City with a Chance.* Milwaukee: The Bruce Publishing Company, 1968.

Bergman, Peter M. *The Chronological History of the Negro in America.* New York: Mentor Books, 1969.

Blackburn, Sara, ed. *White Justice: Black Experiences Today in America's Courtrooms.* New York: Harper & Row, 1971.

Black Panther Sisters Talk about Women's Liberation. Wisconsin State Historical Society Pamphlet Collection, n.d.

Brent, William Lee. *Long Time Gone.* New York: Times Books, 1996.

Brown, Elaine. *A Taste of Power: A Black Woman's Story.* New York: Pantheon Books, 1992.

Cannon, Terry. *All Power to the People: The Story of the Black Panther Party.* San Francisco: Peoples Press, 1970.

Carmichael, Stokely and Hamilton, Charles V. *Black Power: The Politics of Liberation in America.* New York: Vintage Books, 1967.

Carroll, Lee. Hacks, *Blacks and Cons: Race Relations in a Maximum Security Prison.* Lexington, Ky.: Lexington Books, 1974.

Chevigny, Paul. *Cops and Rebels: A Study of Provocation.* New York: Pantheon Books, 1972.

Citizens Research and Investigation Committee & Tackwood, Louis E. *The Glass House Tapes.* New York: Avon Books, 1973.

Clark, Kenneth, ed. *Racism and American Education: A Dialogue and Agenda for Action.* With a foreword by Averell Harriman and an introduction by McGeorge Bundy. New York: Harper & Row, 1970.

Cleaver, Eldridge. *Soul on Ice.* New York: Dell Publishing Inc., 1970.

Cleaver, Kathleen and Katsiaficas, George, eds. *Liberation, Imagination and the Black Panther Party: A New Look at the Panthers and their Legacy*. New York: Routledge, 2001.

Collier, Peter and Horowitz, David. *Destructive Generation: Second Thoughts about the Sixties*. New York: Summit Books, 1989.

Davis, Angela. *Angela Davis: An Autobiography*. New York: International Publishers, 1988.

DeLoach, Cartha. *Hoover's FBI: The Inside Story by Hoover's Trusted Liaison*. Washington D.C.: Regnery Publish, Inc., 1995.

DuBois, W.E.B. *The Souls of Black Folk*. 1903. Reprint, New York: Signet Classic, 1982.

Eisinger, Peter K. *Patterns of Interracial Politics: Conflict and Cooperation in the City*. New York: Academic Press, 1976.

Evans, Sara. *Personal Politics: The Roots of Women's Liberation in the Civil Rights Movement and the New Left*. New York: Vintage Books, 1979.

Fanon, Frantz. *The Wretched of the Earth*. New York: Grove Press, Inc., 1961. Reprint, 1968.

Finkenbine, Roy E. *Sources of the African-American Past: Primary Sources in American History*. New York: Longman Publishers, 1997.

Flaming, Karl & Ong, John. *A Social Report for Milwaukee: Trends and Indicators*. Milwaukee: Milwaukee Urban Observatory, 1973.

Flaming, Karl. *Who 'Riots' and Why?* Milwaukee: Milwaukee Urban League, 1968.

Foner, Philip, ed. *The Black Panthers Speak*. With a foreword by Clayborne Carson. New York: Da Capo Press, 1995.

Genet, Jean. *Prisoner of Love*. Hanover, NH: Wesleyan University Press, 1992.

Gitlin, Todd. *The Sixties: Years of Hope, Days of Rage*. New York: Bantam Books, 1987.

Heath, G. Louis. *The Black Panther Leaders Speak*. Metuchen, N.J.: The Scarecrow Press, 1976.

———, *Off the Pigs!: The History and Literature of the Black Panther Party*. Metuchen, N.J.: The Scarecrow Press, Inc. 1976.

Hill, Norman, ed. *The Black Panther Menace: America's Neo-Nazis*. New York: Popular Library, 1971.

Hilliard, David and Weise, Donald, eds. *The Huey P. Newton Reader*. With a foreword by Fredrika Newton. New York: Seven Stories Press, 2002.

Hilliard, David and Cole, Lewis. *This Side of Glory: The Autobiography of David Hilliard and the Story of the Black Panther Party*. Boston: Little, Brown and Company, 1993.

Hollings, Ernest F. *The Case Against Hunger: A Demand for National Policy*. New York: Cowles Book Co., 1970.

In Search of Common Ground. New York: W.W. Norton & Company, Inc., 1973.

Jackson, George. *Soledad Brother*. New York: Coward-McCann, 1970. Reprint, Chicago: Lawrence Hill Books, 1994.

Jacques-Garvey, Amy, ed. *Philosophies and Opinions of Marcus Garvey*. Vols. 1 & 2, 1923. Reprint, New York: Antheneum, 1977.

Karenga, Maulana. *The Quotable Karenga.* n.d.

King, Martin Luther, Jr. *Why We Can't Wait.* 1964. Reprint, New York: Penguin Books, n.d.

Knoohuizen, Ralph, Fahey, Richard P. & Palmer, Deborah J. *Police and Their Use of Fatal Force in Chicago.* Chicago: 1972.

Lerner, Gerda ed. *Black Women in White America: A Documentary History.* New York: Pantheon Books, 1972. Reprint, New York: Vintage Books, 1973.

Maier, Henry. *The Mayor Who Made Milwaukee Famous.* Lanham, Maryland: Madison Books, 1993.

Marine, Gene. *The Black Panthers.* New York: Harper & Row, 1971.

Moore, Chuck. *I was a Black Panther.* Garden City, NY: Doubleday, 1970.

National Center on Police and Community Relations: A Survey of Police and Community Relations. East Lansing: Michigan State University, 1965.

Newton, Huey. *Revolutionary Suicide.* Harcourt Brace Javonovich, Inc. 1973. Reprint, Writers and Readers Publishing, Inc., 1995.

Newton, Michael. *Bitter Grain: The Story of the Black Panther Party.* Los Angeles: Holloway House, 1980.

Njeri, Akua. *My Life with the Black Panther Party.* Oakland: Burning Spear, 1991.

O'Neill, William. *Coming Apart: An Informal History of America in the 1960s.* Chicago: Quadrangle, 1971.

O'Reilly, Kenneth. *Black Americans: The FBI Files.* New York: Carroll & Graf Publishers, 1994.

———. *Racial Matters: The FBI's Secret File on Black America.* New York: The Free Press, 1989.

Raines, Howell. *My Soul is Rested: Movement Days in the Deep South Remembered.* Ontario, Canada: Longham Canada Unlimited, 1977. Reprint, New York: Penguin Books Inc., 1987.

Report of the National Advisory Commission on Civil Disorders. New York: E.P. Dutton & Company, Inc., 1968.

Schanche, Don A. *The Panther Paradox: A Liberal's Dilemma.* New York: David Mckay Co., 1970.

Schmandt, Henry J., John G. Goldbach and Donald B. Vogel. *Milwaukee: A Contemporary Urban Profile.* New York: Praeger Publishers, 1971.

Schmandt, Henry J. and Harold M. Rose. *Citizen Attitudes in Milwaukee: A Further Look.* Milwaukee: Milwaukee Urban Observatory, 1972.

Seale, Bobby. *Seize the Time: The Story of the Black Panther Party and Huey Newton.* Random House, 1970. Reprint, Baltimore: Black Classic Press, 1991.

Seham, Max. *Blacks and American Medical Care.* Minneapolis: University of Minnesota Press, 1973.

Sellers, Cleveland with Terrell, Robert. *The River of No Return: The Autobiography of a Black Militant and the Life and Death of SNCC.* Jackson: William Morrow & Company, Inc., 1973. Reprint, Jackson: University Press of Mississippi, 1990.

School of Social Work, University of Wisconsin-Madison, *Social Problem Indicators and Related Demographic Characteristics, Milwaukee.* Madison: University of Wisconsin-Madison, 1966.

Shakur, Assata. *Assata: An Autobiography*. Chicago: Lawrence Hill Books, 1987.

Sheehy, Gail. *Panthermania: The Clash of Black against Black in one American City*. New York: Harper & Row, 1971. de Vise, Pierre. *Misused and Misplaced Hospitals and Doctors: A Locational Analysis of the Urban Health Crisis*. Washington D.C.: 1973.

Wallace, Michelle. *Black Macho and the Myth of the Superwoman*. New York: Dial Press, 1978.

Weissman, Steve. *Big Brother and the Holding Company*. Palo Alto, Ca: Ramparts Press, 1974.

Wilkins, Roy with Matthews, Tom. *Standing Fast: The Autobiography of Roy Wilkins*. Viking Press, 1982. Reprint, New York: Penguin Books, 1984.

Wilkins, Roy & Clark, Ramsey. *Search and Destroy: A Report By the Commission of Inquiry*. New York, Metropolitan Applied Research Center, Inc. 1973.

Williams, Julian E. *Black Panthers are not Black . . . They are Red*. Tulsa: Christian Crusade Publications, 1970.

Williams, Robert F. *Negroes With Guns*. With a Foreword by Gloria House and an introduction by Timothy Tyson. New York: Marzani & Munsell, 1962. Reprint, Detroit: Wayne State University Press, 1998.

Woodward, C. Vann. The Strange Career of Jim Crow. New York: Oxford University Press, 1966.

X, Malcolm. *The Autobiography of Malcolm X, as told to Alex Haley*. With an introduction by M.S. Handler. New York: Ballantine Books, 1964. Reprint, Grove Press, 1965.

Youth of the Rural Organizing and Cultural Center. *Minds Stayed on Freedom: The Civil Rights Struggle in the Rural South*. With an introduction by Jay McLeod. Boulder: Westview Press, 1991.

Dissertations

Newton, Huey. "War Against the Panthers: A Study of Repression in America." Ph.D. diss., University of California Santa-Cruz, 1980.

Articles

Calloway, Carolyn R. "Group Cohesiveness in the Black Panther Party." *Journal of Black Studies* 8 (September 1977): 55–74.

Campbell, Dick. "Sickle-cell Anemia and its Effect of Black People." *Crisis* 78, no. 1 (1971): 7–9.

Karenga, Ron. "Some Preliminary Notes." *Black Scholar* 6, no. 5 (1975), 23–30.

Munford, Clarence J. "The Fallacy of Lumpen Ideology." *Black Scholar* 4 (July-August 1973): 47–51.

"Freedom News." *Crisis* 74, no. 10 (1967): 492.

"The Police and The Negro Community." *Crisis* 75, no. 7 (1968): 223–225.

"The Police Versus the Black Panthers." Crisis 77, no. 1 (1970): 23–25.

"White Tigers Versus Black Panthers." Crisis 75, no. 8 (1968): 276.

Videocassettes & DVD's

Ain't Gonna Shuffle No More, vol. 11, Eyes on the Prize. Produced and directed by Sam Pollard and Sheila Bernard. 60 min. Blackside, 1990. Videocassette.

A Nation of Law?, vol. 12, Eyes on the Prize. Produced and directed by Terry Kay Rockefeller, Thomas Orr and Louis J. Massiah. 60 min. Blackside, 1990. Videocassette.

A Place of Rage. Produced and Directed by Pratibha Parmar. 60 min. Women Make Movies, 1991. Videocassette.

Back to the Movement, vol. 14, Eyes on the Prize. Produced and directed by Davis Lacy, Jr. & James Devinney. 60 min. Blackside, 1990. Videocassette.

Berkeley in the Sixties. Produced and Directed by Mark Kitchel. 117 min. First Run Features, 1990. DVD.

Power!, vol. 9, Eyes on the Prize. Produced and directed by Louis J. Massiah and Terry Kay Rockefeller. 60 min. Blackside, 1990. Videocassette.

Secondary Sources

Books

Branch, Taylor. *Parting the Waters: America in the King Years, 1954–1963*. New York: Touchstone Books, 1989.

———. *Pillar of Fire: America in the King Years, 1963–1965*. New York: Simon & Schuster, 1998.

Burner, David. *Making Peace with the Sixties*. Princeton: Princeton University Press, 1996.

Carson, Clayborne. *In Struggle: SNCC and the Black Awakening of the 1960's*. Cambridge: Harvard University Press, 1981.

Chalmers, David. *And the Crooked Places Made Straight*. Baltimore: Johns Hopkins Press, 1991.

Churchill, Ward & Vander Wall, Jim. *Agents of Repression: The FBI's Secret Wars Against the Black Panther Party and the American Indian Movement*. Boston, South End Press, 1988. Reprint, Boston, South End Press, 1990.

Citizens Board of Inquiry into Hunger and Malnutrition in the United States. *Hunger U.S.A. Revisited*. n.d.

Clarke, Edwin & Steve Paulson, with an introduction by Belden Paulson. *The Harambee Health Experiment*. University of Wisconsin-Extension: Center for Urban Community Development, 1983.

Cohen, Robert Carl. *Black Crusader: A Biography of Robert Franklin Williams*. Secaucus, New Jersey, Lyle Stuart Inc., 1972.

Coleman, Jonathan. *Long Way to Go: Black and White in America*. New York: Atlantic Monthly Press, 1997.

Collier-Thomas, Bettye and V.P. Franklin. *Sisters in the Struggle: African American Women in the Civil Rights-Black Power Movement*. New York: New York University Press, 2001.

Cruden, Robert. *The Negro in Reconstruction*. Englewood Cliffs, NJ: Prentice-Hall, 1969.

Davis, Lenwood, ed. *Daddy Grace: An Annotated Biography*. New York: Greenwood Press, 1992.

Diggins, John Patrick. *The Rise and Fall of the American Left*. New York: W. W. Norton & Company, 1992.

Dittmer, John. *Local People: The Struggle for Civil Rights in Mississippi*. Urbana: University of Illinois Press, 1994.

Donner, Frank. *Protectors of Privilege: Red Squads and Police Repression in Urban America*. Berkeley: University of California Press, 1990.

D'Orso, Michael. *Like Judgment Day: The Ruin and Redemption of a Town called Rosewood*. New York: G.P. Putnam's Sons, 1996.

Egerton, John. *Speak Now Against the Day: The Generation Before the Civil Rights Movement in the South*. Chapel Hill: University of North Carolina Press, 1994.

George, John and Wilcox, Laird. *Nazis, Communists, Klansmen and Others on the Fringe: Political Extremism in America*. Buffalo: Prometheus Books, 1992.

Giddings, Paula. *When and Where I Enter: The Impact of Black Women on Race and Sex in America*. New York: W. Morrow, 1984. Reprint, New York: Bantam Books, 1988.

Grant, JoAnne. *Ella Baker: Freedom Bound*. New York: John Wiley & Sons, 1998.

Gruberg, Martin. *A Case Study in US Urban Leadership: The Incumbency of Milwaukee Mayor Henry Maier*. Aldershot, England: Avebury, 1996.

Harris, Sara. *Father Divine*. With an introduction by John Henrik Clarke. Double Day & Co., 1953. Reprint, New York: Collier Books, 1971.

Hill, Lance. *The Deacons for Defense: Armed Resistance and the Civil Rights Movement*. Chapel Hill: University of North Carolina Press, 2004.

Jones, Charles E., ed. *The Black Panther Party: Reconsidered*. Baltimore: Black Classic Press, 1998.

Kelly, Robin D.G. *Hammer and Hoe: Alabama Communists During the Great Depression*. Chapel Hill: University of North Carolina Press, 1990.

Lewis, Rupert and Bryan, Patrick, eds. *Garvey: His Work and Impact*. Trenton, New Jersey: African World Press, Inc., 1991.

Meier, August and Rudwick, Elliot. *From Plantation to Ghetto*. 3rd ed. New York: Hill and Wang, 1976. Reprint, New York: Hill and Wang, 1996.

McMillen, Neil. *Dark Journey: Black Mississippians in the Age of Jim Crow*. Urbana: University of Illinois Press, 1989.

McPherson, James. *The Negro's Civil War: How American Blacks Felt and Acted During the War from the Union*. New York: Ballantine Books, 1965. Reprint, Pantheon Books, 1982.

Pearson, Hugh. *The Shadow of the Panther: Huey Newton and the Price of Black Power in America*. Addison-Wesley Publishing Co., Reading, Mass. 1994.

Pfeffer, Paula F. *A. Philip Randolph: Pioneer of the Civil Rights Movement*. Baton Rouge: Louisiana State University Press, 1990.

Ralph, James R. *Northern Protest: Martin Luther King, Jr., Chicago and the Civil Rights Movement*. Cambridge: Harvard University Press, 1994.

Robnett, Belinda. *How Long? How Long?: African American Women in the Struggle for Civil Rights*. Oxford: Oxford University Press, 1997.

Rosengarten, Theodore. *All God's Dangers: The Life of Nate Shaw*. New York: Avon Books, 1974.

Schaefer, Richard T. *Racial and Ethnic Groups*. 4th ed. Harper Collins Publishers, 1990.

Shapiro, Herbert. *White Violence and Black Response: From Reconstruction to Montgomery*. Amherst: University of Massachusetts Press, 1988.

Smallwood, Arwin D. *The Atlas of African-American History and Politics: From the Slave Trade to Modern Times*. Boston: McGraw-Hill, 1998.

Smith, Alice. *The History of Wisconsin, From Exploration to Statehood*. Madison: State Historical Society of Wisconsin, 1973.

Social Development Commission. *Children in Poverty: The State of Milwaukee's Children*. Milwaukee: n.d.

Stein, Judith. *The World of Marcus Garvey: Race and Class in Modern Society*. Baton Rouge: Louisiana State Press, 1986. Reprint, 1991.

Trotter, Joe. *Black Milwaukee: The Making of an Industrial Proletariat, 1915–1945*. Urbana: University of Illinois Press, 1985.

Tyson, Timothy B. *Radio Free Dixie: Robert F. Williams and the Roots of the Black Power Movement*. Chapel Hill: University of North Carolina Press, 1999.

Van Deburg, William L. *New Day in Babylon*. Chicago: The University of Chicago Press, 1992.

Vincent, Theodore G. *Black Power and The Garvey Movement*. Berkeley: The Ramparts Press, n.d.

Watts, Jill. *God, Harlem U.S.A.: The Father Divine Story*. Berkeley: University of California Press, 1992. Reprint, 1995.

Weisbrot, Robert. *Father Divine and the Struggle for Racial Equality*. Urbana: University of Illinois Press, 1983.

Williams, Lee and Williams, Lee II. *Anatomy of Four Race Riots: Racial Conflict in Knoxville, Elaine (Arkansas), Tulsa and Chicago*. With a foreword by Roy Wilkins. Oxford: University and College Press of Mississippi, 1972.

Wood, John A. *The Panthers and the Militias: Brothers Under the Skin?* Lanham, MD: University Press of America, 2002.

Videocassettes

Higher Learning. Produced and directed by John Singleton. 127 min. Columbia Pictures, 1995. Videocassette.

I Remember Harlem: The Depression Years, 1930–1940. Produced and directed by William Miles. 57 min. Films for the Humanities and Sciences, 1991. Videocassette.

Panther. Produced and directed by Mario Van Peebles and Melvin Van Peebles. Gramercy, 1994. Videocassette.

Rosewood. Produced by Jon Peters and directed by John Singleton. 120 min. Warner Brothers, 1997. Videocassette.

The Sixties, part 2. Produced and directed by Jim Chorry. 120 min. National Broadcasting Company Studios, 1999. Videocassette.

Theses and Dissertations

Braun, Mark. "Social Change and the Empowerment of the Poor: Poverty Representation." Ph.D. diss., University of Wisconsin-Milwaukee, 1999.

Snyder, Ronald. "Chief for Life: Harold Breier and his Era." PhD diss., University of Wisconsin-Milwaukee, 2002.

Wendelberger, Jay, "The Open-Housing Movement in Milwaukee: Hidden Transcripts of the Urban Poor." M.A. thesis, University of Wisconsin-Milwaukee, 1996.

White, Miriam. "The Black Panther's Free Breakfast for Children Program." M.A. thesis, University of Wisconsin-Madison, 1988.

Articles

Dalfiume, Richard. "The 'Forgotten Years' of the Negro Revolution." *Journal of American History* 60, no. 1 (1968): 90–106.

Ngozi-Brown, Scot. "The Us Organization, Maulana Karenga, and Conflict with the Black Panther Party." *Journal of Black Studies* 28, no. 2 (1997): 157–170.

Sitkoff, Harvard. "Racial Militancy and Interracial Violence in the Second World War." *Journal of American History* 58, no. 3 (1971): 661–681.

Tyson, Tim. "Robert F. Williams, 'Black Power,' and the Roots of the African American Freedom Struggle." *Journal of American History* 85, no. 2 (1998): 544–570.

Web Sites

www.hungertaskforce.org/all_about.htm
www.hungertaskforce.org/Bringing_Food/index.html
www.hungertaskforce.org/Graphics/Documents/htf_annual_report04.pdf
www.hungertaskforce.org/index.htm
www.jsonline.com/news/editorials/feb05/304885.asp
www.jsonline.com/news/metro/apr05/318760.asp
www.jsonline.com/new/metro/jun05/332631.asp
www.jsonline.com/news/metro/mar05/313860.asp
www.jsonline.com/news/metro/may05/327952.asp

Information Sources

Humphrey, Liz. Coordinator of Hunger Task Force Special Events. Phone message left by Humphrey on author's answering machine, 28 June 1999.

Wisconsin State Legislative Reference Bureau, 608–266–0341.

Index

A

Abernathy, Ralph, 20
Abron, JoNina, 9
American Indian Movement (AIM), 8
Andrews, Byron, 91
Anthony, Earl, 9
Anti-war Movement, 6, 27
Armed Self-Defense, 2, 7, 13–23
Armour, Norma, 9
Asian American Movement, 27
Assembly Bill 42, 60
Atlanta Riot (1906), 15

B

Barbee, Lloyd, 47
Bartlett, John, 92
Bates, Daisy, 22
Bellamy, Nate, 51, 58, 82
Black Militias, 13–14
Black Panther, 9, 38
Black Panther Militia, 1, 7; and Michael
    McGee, *see* Michael McGee
    Black Panther Party, 1–14, 23,
    25, 27–39, 50–55, 57–70, 71–77,
    79, 81–89, 92–93; and *Black
    Panther, see Black Panther*; and
    Boston branch, 38; and Brooklyn
    branch, 36; and Chicago branch,
    10, 31, 33–36; and Cleveland
    branch, 37; and coalitions, 2, 8,
    51, 54, 59; and community pro-
    grams and services, 1–2, 7, 9, 11,
    23, 25, 31, 34–39, 53, 57–69,
    71–77, 79, 84–86, 92–93; and
    Denzil Dowell case, 33; and Des

Moines branch, 31; and Federal
    Bureau of Investigation (FBI),
    see FBI; flaws of, 11, 81–86;
    founding of, 28; growth of,
    29, 50; and historiography of,
    2–4; and ideology, 1, 5–10, 23,
    28–29, 33, 38, 50–51, 65, 84;
    and Kansas City branch, 35–36;
    and Los Angeles branch, 31, 35,
    88; and Memphis branch, 39;
    and Milwaukee branch, *see* Mil-
    waukee branch of the Black Pan-
    ther Party; misperceptions of,
    1–6, 8, 11–12, 29, 34, 57, 89;
    and New Haven branch, 9, 35;
    and New York chapter, 39; and
    Oakland branch, 31, 35, 37–39;
    and Philadelphia branch, 36, 38
    ; and police repression, 10, 31,
    33–34, 51–54, 87; and role of
    women in, 8–10, 54, 73–74, 86;
    and Sacramento branch, 31; and
    San Francisco branch, 37; and
    San Jose branch, 37; and Seattle
    branch, 37–38; and self-defense,
    2–3, 5, 7, 14, 23, 32, 50; and
    sexism, 8–10, 73–74, 86; and
    Staten Island branch, 36–37;
    and whites, 2, 5–6, 59
Black Power Movement, 5, 28
Blackstone Rangers, 31
Bond, Julian, 21
Breier, Harold, 11, 43, 45, 47, 54, 58–60, 91
    Brown Berets, 8, 59
Brown, Elaine, 8–9

149

C

Camp Hill, Alabama (1931), 16
Carmichael, Stokely, 31
Carter, Alprentice, 30
Cheney, James, 7, 22
Chesser, Walter, 51, 57, 79, 83
Chicano Movement, 27
Citizens for Central City School Breakfast
        Program (CCCSBP), 75–77
Civil Rights Movement, 7, 18, 20, 27- 28, 32
Clark, Mark, 33
Clarke, David, 91
Cleaver, Kathleen, 9
Coggs, Isaac, 47
Coggs, Velma, 49
Collins, Booker, 50, 52
Committee of 21, 66
Congress of Racial Equality (CORE), 21,
        47–48; and Freedom Riders,
        Counterculture, 27
Crawford, Allen, 53
Crayton, Paul, 73
Criminal Justice Reform Act of 1975, 67
Cross Lutheran Church, 72–75, 84–85; and
        Joseph Ellwanger, *see* Joseph
        Ellwanger
Crittenden, Will, 85

D

Daddy Grace, 23–24
Davis, Angela, 8–9, 28
Davis, Antonio, 91
Deacons for Self-Defense and Justice, 7,
        22–23
DuBois, David, 67
DuBois, W.E.B., 15

E

Elaine, Arkansas (1919), 15
Ellwanger, Joseph, 73–75, 78, 84–85
Epps, Lynn, 65
Evers, Medgar, 18

F

Fanon, Frantz, 28
Father Divine, 23–24
Federal Bureau of Investigation (FBI), 2,
        4, 12, 29–31, 50, 53–54; and
        Counter- Intelligence Program
        (COINTELPRO), 4, 30; and
        Freedom of Information Act, 12
Fort, Jeff, 31

Fultz, Michael, 10

G

Garvey, Marcus, 24
Gay Liberation Movement, 27
Gentry, Dakin, 7, 51, 58, 65, 72, 81–84
Gitlin, Todd, 8
Glover, Alfonzo, 92
Goodman, Andrew, 7, 22
Gray, Ralph, 16
Great Migration, 42
Groppi, James, 43, 48–49

H

Halyard (Clark), Ardie, 47
Halyard, Wilbur, 47
Hampton, Fred, 10, 33–35
Harambee Health Task Force, 64
Hegerty, Nannette, 91
Henry, Robert, 91–92
Hilliard, David, 33, 72
Hoover, J. Edgar, 4, 29
Huggins, Ericka, 9
Huggins, John, 30
Hunger Hike, 61–62
Hunger Task Force of Milwaukee (HTFM),
        11, 71, 77–79, 92–93
Hutton, Bobby, 33

I

Isaac Coggs Community Health Center, 64

J

Jackson, George, 27
Jackson, Phyllis, 9
Jackson State University (1970), 32
Jenkins, Larry, 92
Jennings, Regina, 10
Jones, Arthur, 91
Jude, Frank, 92

K

Karenga, Maulana, 8, 30, 39
Kelley, Joan, 9
Kerner Commission, 29, 32
King, Martin Luther, Jr., 18–19, 21, 27
King, Yvonne, 9
Ku Klux Klan, 13, 22, 49

L

Lacy, Ernest, 60
Lafayette, Bernard, 22

Levrettes, Earl, 52
Lins, Fred, 47–48
Lovetta X, 50, 81–85
Lynching, 14–15

M
Maier, Henry, 11, 43, 50
Malcolm X, 22
Matthews, Connie, 9
Maxie, Roy, 77
McClain, Joe, 42–43, 49, 51, 82–84
McDowell, Calvin, 14
McGee, Geneva, 64
McGee, Michael, 1, 7, 45, 53–54, 61–62,
      68, 77, 86
McKissick, Clifford, 44
Milwaukee: African American Freedom
      Struggle in, 11, 42–43, 47–50;
      Congress of Racial Equality
      (CORE) in, 47–48; early history,
      41–42 ; hunger in, 71–72, 74,
      90, 92–93; National Association
      for the Advancement of Col-
      ored People (NAACP) in, 42,
      47–49; open-housing marches,
      49; police brutality, *see* police
      brutality; riot in, 44–46; and
      Youth Commandos, *see* Youth
      Commandos
Milwaukee Branch of the Black Panther
      Party, 7, 10–12, 36, 50–55,
      57–69, 71, 77, 79, 81–89,
      92–93; and Breakfast for Chil-
      dren Program, 11, 36, 53, 69,
      71- 77, 79, 84–86; and Busing
      to Prisons Program, 57, 61–62;
      and coalitions, 51, 54, 59; and
      community programs in general,
      11, 57, 64–69; dissolved, 53,
      58, 88, 92–93; and FBI, *see* FBI;
      flaws of, 11, 81–86; founding
      of, 50, 59, 88; and medical care,
      57, 62- 64; and Michael McGee,
      see Michael McGee; Milwaukee
      Three, *see* Milwaukee Three;
      and People's Committee for
      Survival, *see* People's Commit-
      tee for Survival; and People's
      Free Health Center *see* People's
      Free Health Center; and police
      decentralization plan, 57–60;
      and police repression, 51–54,
      87; and role of women in, 50,
      54, 73–74, 86; sexism in, 10,
      73–74, 86
Milwaukee Three, 52, 61, 81–82
Milwaukee United School Integration Com-
      mittee (MUSIC), 48
Montgomery Bus Boycott, 18
Moss, Thomas, 14

N
Nadir, 14
National Association for the Advancement
      of Colored People (NAACP),
      8, 18–20, 22, 32, 42, 47–49,
      88; and Youth Commandos,
      see Youth Commandos; and
      Youth Council, 22, 48, 49, 88;
      National Committee to Combat
      Fascism, 59
Nation of Islam, 8, 23–25, 54
National Organization for Women, (NOW),
      8
Negroes with Guns, 20, 28
Newton, Huey, 5–6, 28–29, 33, 37, 54, 88
New York City Draft Riot (1863), 13
Nixon, E.D., 18

O
Oasis Theater, 64–65
Organization of Organizations (Triple O),
      64
Orangeburg, South Carolina (1968) 32,
      Owens, George, 53

P
Parks, Rosa, 18
Peace and Freedom Party (PFP), 2
People's Committee to Free Jan Starks, 53
People's Committee for Survival, 53, 61- 64,
      76–77
People's Free Health Center, 57, 62–64
Police Brutality, 1, 3, 28, 31–33, 43–47,
      57–58, 60–61, 66, 91–92
Prado, Wilbert, 92

R
Randolph, A. Philip, 5
Reconstruction, 13–14
Red Book, 84
Red Power, 27
Red Squad, 54, 86
Reuss, Henry, 53, 67

Robinson, JoAnne, 19
Rodriguez, Samuel, 92
Rosewood, Florida (1923), 15–16
Rush, Bobby, 35
Rustin, Bayard, 19

S
Saint Augustine, Florida, 22
Salahadyn, Abdullah, 84
Seale, Bobby, 28, 33, 35, 88
Schwerner, Michael, 7, 22
Sharecropping Unions, 15–17
Shaw, Nate, 17
Shuttlesworth, Fred, 20
Sims, Charles R., 7, 23
Southern Christian Leadership Conference
            (SCLC), 20–21
Starks, Jan, 53
Starks, Ronald, 50, 53, 58, 60–61, 65, 83
Stewart, Henry, 14
Students for a Democratic Society (SDS), 2,
            8, 54, 59
Student Non-violent Coordinating Committee
            (SNCC), 6, 8, 21–22, 31, 88; and
            Freedom Summer, 6, 21
Summerfest, 92
Survival Programs, *see also* Black Panther
            Party; community programs and
            services
Sweet, Ossian 16

T
Tackwood, Louis E., 30
Trenton, John, 85

Tubman, Harriet 13
Turnbow, Hartman, 21

U
United Black Community Council (UBCC), 54
Universal Negro Improvement Association
            (UNIA), 24
Us, 4, 8, 30, 39

V
Vietnam, 27; and African
Americans, 50

W
Welch, Felix, 52, 82
Wells, Ida B., 14–15
White, Jesse, 52, 65, 81–82
White, Walter, 17–18
Williams, Robert F., 19–20, 28, 88
Williamson, Kenneth, 53
Wilkins, Roy, 20, 27, 34
Wisconsin Committee to Combat
Fascism (WCCF), 59
Women's Movement, 27
Women's Political Council, 19
World War II; and African
Americans, 19, 23
Wretched of the Earth, 28

Y
Young, Donald, 50
Young Lords, 59
Youth Commandos, 42, 49–50, 82–83
Youth International Party (Yippies), 2